IMAGES
of America

BOZEMAN

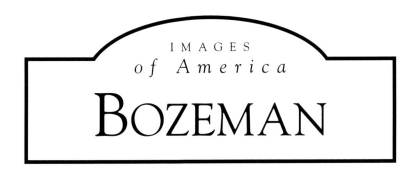

IMAGES
of America

BOZEMAN

Denise Glaser Malloy
and the Pioneer Museum of Bozeman

ARCADIA
PUBLISHING

Published by Arcadia Publishing
Charleston SC, Chicago IL, Portsmouth NH, San Francisco CA

Printed in the United States of America

Library of Congress Catalog Card Number: 2007936581

For all general information contact Arcadia Publishing at:
Telephone 843-853-2070
Fax 843-853-0044
E-mail sales@arcadiapublishing.com
For customer service and orders:
Toll-Free 1-888-313-2665

Visit us on the Internet at www.arcadiapublishing.com

*To Sam and Max, who amaze me each day,
and to Bob, who makes it all possible.*

CONTENTS

ACKNOWLEDGMENTS

Projects of this magnitude are rarely the result of the efforts of an individual. This book is no exception. Many thanks to the Gallatin Historical Society and the Pioneer Museum of Bozeman and museum executive director John C. Russell, who gave me access to the photographic archives and the museum's extensive collection of research materials and for sharing his expertise. I am deeply indebted to you, and I am grateful for your generosity. A special thank you is due to assistant museum director Ann Butterfield, whose boundless enthusiasm for history and sense of humor made this project a pleasure. She selflessly gave of her time and shared her vast knowledge. This book could have never happened without her. Ann made it a delight every step of the way.

I am also grateful for the expert guidance from Hannah Carney, my editor at Arcadia Publishing. Her wisdom, advice, and encouragement helped this project progress smoothly from start to finish. I am particularly appreciative of her reminders to always backup my documents. Thankfully, I listened.

I am especially thankful that this wonderful community recognized the importance of and worked so diligently to preserve the pieces of Bozeman's history. Volunteers at the museum have spent countless hours devoted to the preservation of the photographs and written documentation of the growth and change of Bozeman over the years. These volunteers, who give their time and knowledge in the spirit of preserving the past, should be commended for their efforts to insure that the rich tapestry of Bozeman's history is preserved for generations to come.

Unless otherwise noted, all photographs in this book came from the archives of the Pioneer Museum of Bozeman.

INTRODUCTION

The Gallatin Valley's first inhabitants were Native Americans who hunted the region for hundreds of years. The Lewis and Clark expedition passed through the valley in 1805 and recorded its first written description. Industrious mountain men such as Jim Bridger led trapping expeditions through the region. After the discovery of gold in the 1860s, the area truly began its rapid growth.

John Bozeman, the town's namesake, and explorer John Jacobs searched for a shorter route from the east to reach the mining camps near Virginia City and traveled much the same route as William Clark. After the successful passage into the Gallatin Valley, the Bozeman Trail became the primary route for wagon trains entering the valley from the east.

Although many of the early settlers lived in Gallatin City, just west of Bozeman, a few individuals decided to establish their residence in the southeastern portion of the valley on a fork of the East Gallatin River. On July 7, 1864, William Beall and Daniel Rouse filed the first land claims. By the end of 1864, the town of Bozeman had several cabins, a hotel, and a few shops to supply travelers on their westward journey as well as offer provisions for inhabitants of the growing town.

Although originally established to provide protection for residents of the Gallatin Valley from Native American attack, Fort Ellis, in reality, proved to be more of an economic boon to the town. Years of bloody and fierce fighting on the Bozeman Trail generated a fear of attacks on the new settlement. When a Sioux killed two men near Bozeman Pass in 1865, residents assumed their worst fears had now been confirmed and pleaded with the government for help. But after Thomas Cover reported that John Bozeman was murdered by Blackfeet Indians in April 1867, the outcry for protection was loud and clear. Public sentiment prompted officials to establish this military post complete with a 10-foot-high stockade where residents could flee if attacked. But the possibility of attacks quickly diminished and the stockade was soon removed. The military post at Fort Ellis then served to bolster the Bozeman economy rather than provide refuge.

Soldiers from the fort also provided military escorts for explorers and early tourists crossing Native American land to reach Bozeman and the Yellowstone region. The Folsom Expedition of 1869, the Washburn Expedition of 1870, and the Hayden Expedition of 1871 all mustered at Fort Ellis. The first expedition to what would later become the country's first national park, Yellowstone, also left from the fort.

Farmers and ranchers who arrived found the Gallatin Valley provided fertile land for crops and grazing. The rich soil and excellent growing conditions caused enthusiastic farmers to dub the region the "Egypt of America." In 1865, the valley had approximately 1,500 acres planted with wheat that produced over 20,000 bushels. By 1867, nearly 8,400 acres were planted in wheat.

Although prospectors near Bozeman did not find bountiful deposits of gold as in nearby Virginia City, they focused on a new-found discovery that would prove to be equally valuable: coal. Just east of Bozeman, small towns quickly sprang up as mining operations thrived. With the advent of the coke oven, coal was transformed into a material that would burn hot enough to smelt ore. This would ultimately help fuel the copper industry in nearby Butte.

As the railroad expanded operations into the area in the 1880s, it brought not only jobs but also the opportunity for easier passage to the Gallatin Valley. Businessmen in southwestern Montana successfully lobbied to bring the Northern Pacific Railroad route to southern Montana rather than the through the northern part of the state as originally suggested by the survey. Completing the route over the Bozeman Pass was a technical feat given the rugged terrain. Tons of rock and earth were moved and a tunnel created in the final phase linking the east and west in the northern United States. Once finished, the Northern Pacific Railroad stretched from the shores of Lake Superior to Puget Sound in Washington State. The railroad also expanded the growing coal mining industry and gave the agricultural products a ready access to market.

As the town of Bozeman grew in the early 1880s, it had hotels, general stores, and a host of specialty shops. As the town grew, many successful businesses lined Main Street in the early 1900s, some of which are still in operation today. Saloons, billiards halls, and restaurants offered entertainment. Several of the original brick buildings in downtown Bozeman remain today as a testament to the early, thriving town. Although the town unsuccessfully vied for the title of state capital, it was awarded the area's first land grant college, the Agricultural College of the State of Montana, which opened in 1893.

Bozeman has long held festivals and events as a source of civic pride. Many festivals and celebrations were also conceived as a way to promote tourism in the area. In 1906, the Bozeman Commercial Club created the Sweet Pea Carnival in an effort to draw tourists. Organizers hoped the festival would develop a reputation on a level that would compete with Mardi Gras in New Orleans and the Rose Festival in Portland. August was chosen as the time for the carnival, since the sweet peas would be in full bloom and the weather was typically pleasant. The town's entire population of 4,000 planted and tended to the sweet peas, which were used as decorations all over town. Festivities, which were presided over by the Sweet Pea queen, included a parade, dances, and a baseball game.

The Bozeman Roundup began in 1919 and showcased rodeo cowboys and cowgirls, Native Americans in full tribal regalia, and a presiding queen. The Roundup was part of the national rodeo circuit that featured competitions for a cash prize purse. The spirit of the old West was exemplified by the rowdy and rollicking good time at the Roundup, which was held annually until 1926.

The remarkable environment of the Bozeman area provided the opportunity for many year-round recreational activities, including fishing, skiing, hunting, and camping trips. With Yellowstone National Park located nearby, tourists and locals alike traveled to enjoy the natural wonders of the area.

The colorful history and majestic beauty of Bozeman and the surrounding Gallatin Valley has entranced settlers and visitors over the years and continues to do so to this very day. Indeed, many visitors today report that they were compelled to return to the area, and some relocate here after being captivated by the magnificent scenery surrounding the valley. No doubt, Bozeman has been and remains one of the crown jewels of "the Last Best Place" in Montana.

One

THE LURE OF THE WEST

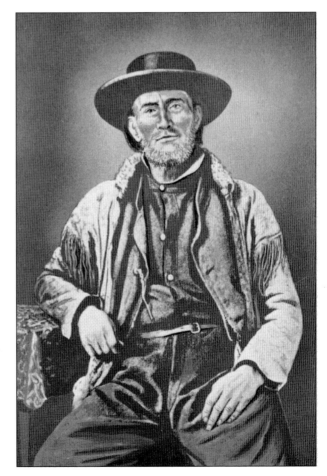

Jim Bridger was a true mountain man who began his first journey westward at the age of 18 as a part of William Ashley's expedition. While Meriwether Lewis and William Clark were some of first non–Native American visitors to the area, Bridger explored the area extensively and guided many pioneers to the Gallatin Valley. (C. M. Ismert etching.)

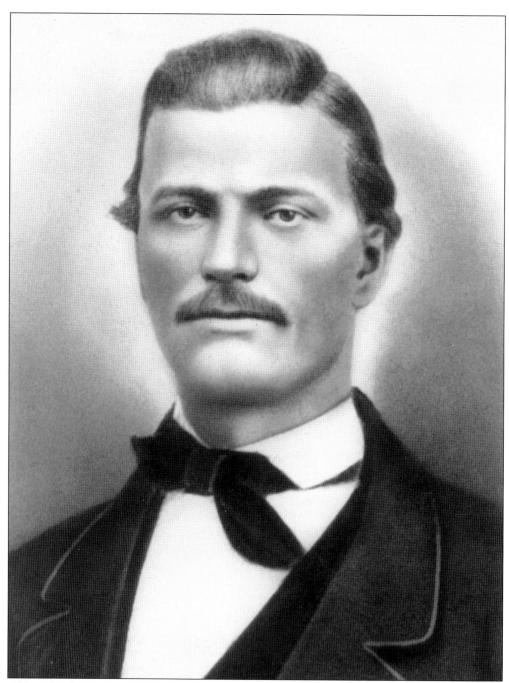

Although John Bozeman originally traveled west in search of gold, he later guided wagon trains as they journeyed westward. On August 9, 1864, he was one of roughly a dozen settlers of the Upper East Gallatin who came together and formed the town of Bozeman. In April 1867, Bozeman and Tom Cover traveled east to Fort Smith to pursue yet another business venture. A few days later, Cover claimed that Bozeman had been killed by Blackfeet Indians. The site was inspected, but no evidence was found. Some believed that Cover was jealous of his wife's interest in Bozeman and killed him. The circumstances of his death have never been fully explained.

Daniel Elliott Rouse was an avid traveler and farmer who had lived all over the United States. He came to the area called Gallatin City in 1862. Rouse also had helped plat other settlements around the country and was instrumental in platting the new town of Bozeman. Rouse helped build the first house in Bozeman in 1864.

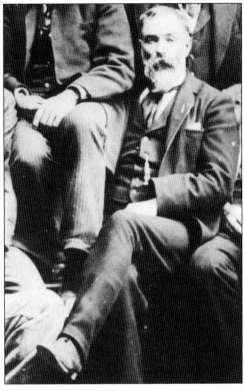

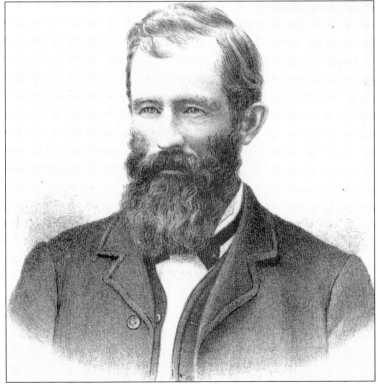

William J. Beall was a farmer and trained architect who traveled the United States before settling in the Bozeman area. Beall built his home, one of the first in Bozeman, just north of Main Street. (Etching from Michael Leeson: *History of Montana*, 1885.)

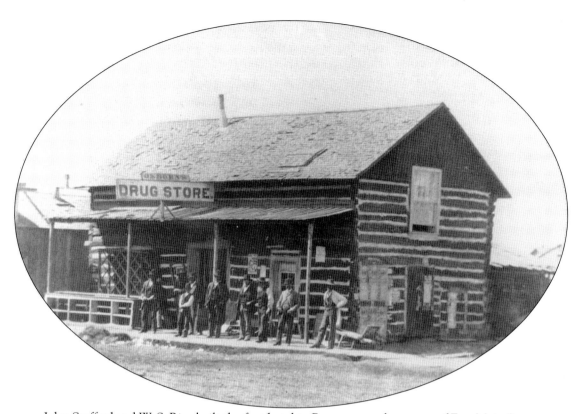

John Stafford and W. S. Rice built the first hotel in Bozeman on the corner of East Main Street and Bozeman Avenue during the summer of 1864. It was later a general store and then became Osborn's Drug Store.

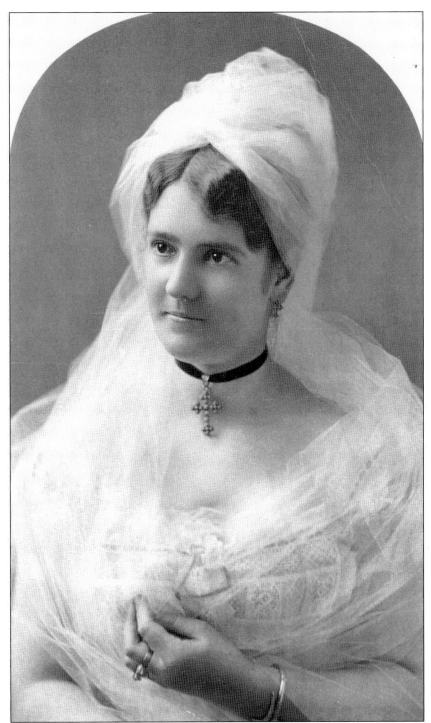

Mary Hunter was born in 1859 and arrived in the Gallatin Valley with her father, Dr. Andrew Hunter, and family in August 1864. Mary Hunter married Lt. Gustavus Doane in 1878 and lived at Fort Ellis for a time. Lieutenant Doane died in 1892, and Mary never remarried. In 1894, she moved back to Bozeman, where she lived until her death in 1952.

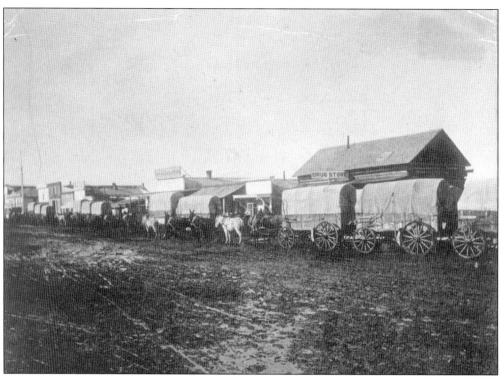

After the town of Bozeman was established, it grew quickly. Here early Main Street is pictured.

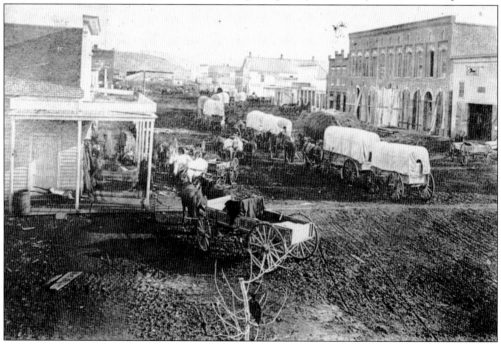

By 1872, Main Street had grown to a sizable downtown providing goods and services for the incoming pioneers and the growing population. Wagon trains arriving in Bozeman line the busy downtown.

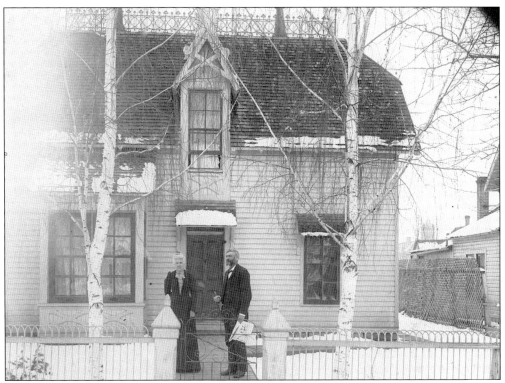

James Lewis and Eleanor Wadsworth Patterson are pictured in front of 209 South Tracy Avenue. This elegant home was built by barber Sam Lewis in 1878.

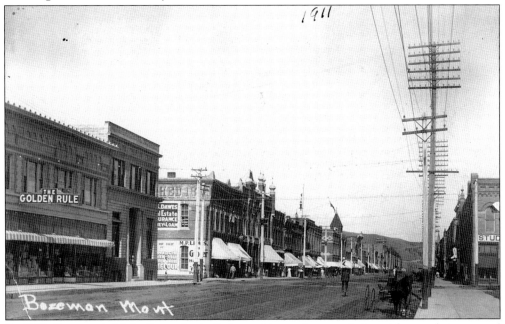

By 1911, Bozeman's Main Street had all the makings of a grand city with paved streets and sidewalks. The grand architecture of early Bozeman remains intact today and adds character to the vibrant downtown.

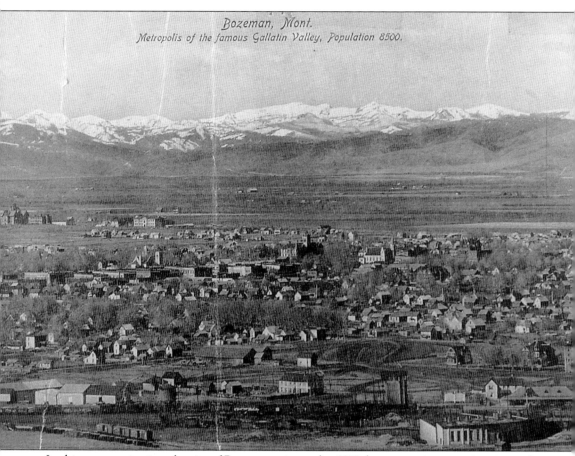

Bozeman, Mont.
Metropolis of the famous Gallatin Valley, Population 8500.

In this panoramic view, the city of Bozeman, pictured c. 1910, has grown into a major city in the Gallatin Valley with a population of 8,500.

Two

TO PROTECT AND SERVE

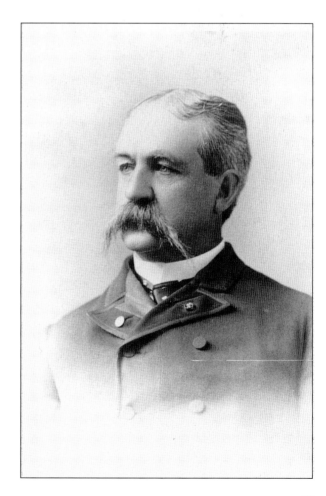

Lt. G. C. Doane, pictured *c.* 1890, was a member of the first battalion of troops coming to Fort Ellis in 1869. Later Doane led the 19 members of the Doane-Washburn exploration party, which left from Fort Ellis in 1870. The party traveled through dense forests up the Yellowstone River to explore the strange reports of boiling springs, erupting pools of water, odd smelling air, and enormous waterfalls.

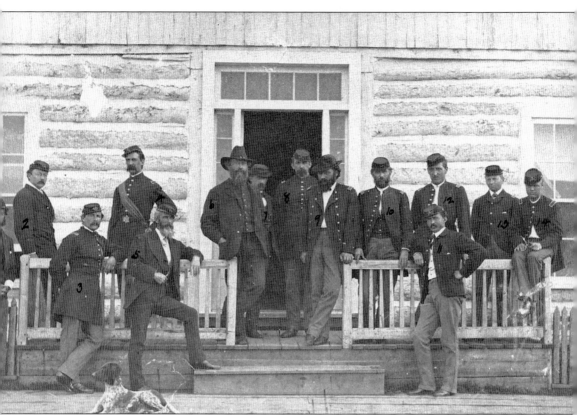

When director of the Geological Survey of the Territories, Ferdinand Hayden, learned of the Washburn-Doane Yellowstone explorations, he garnered Congressional funds for further investigation. Hayden took photographer William Henry Jackson and artist Thomas Moran on the journey, both of whom produced many well-known photographs and sketches of the never-before-seen Yellowstone region. Fort Ellis officers are pictured after their 1871 trip with Hayden to explore the Yellowstone region. Doane, pictured on the left wearing a sash, was the officer of the day. Because of these explorations, Yellowstone National Park was established on March 1, 1872, as the nation's first national park. (Photograph by William Henry Jackson.)

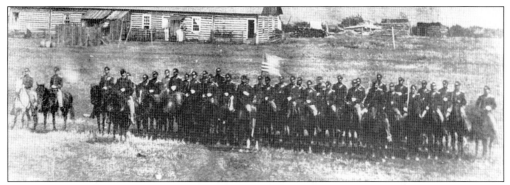

The construction of Fort Ellis originally included a 10-foot log stockade around the fort's perimeter as a place for Gallatin Valley residents to flee in case of Native American attacks. By 1869, the threat of attack had greatly diminished, and the stockade was no longer needed for protection, so the wall was removed. By 1870, over 400 soldiers lived at Fort Ellis. The 2nd Cavalry, Troop F is pictured at Fort Ellis around 1874. The fort played a significant role in the local economy until it closed in 1886.

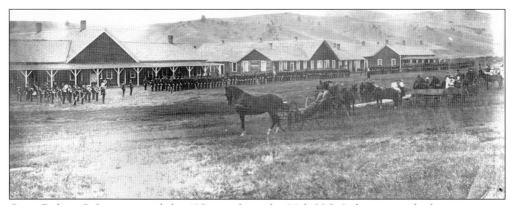

Capt. Robert S. Lamotte and the 195 men from the 30th U.S. Infantry marched into town on August 27, 1867, with the mission of establishing Fort Ellis about three miles east of Bozeman, the fourth and final fort to be built along the Bozeman Trail. The fort's namesake, Col. Augustus Van Horne Ellis, had been killed in the Battle of Gettysburg in 1863 and had never traveled west.

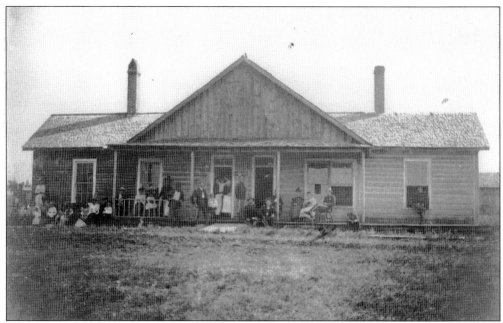

The officers' quarters were quite the contrast to enlisted men's living arrangements. While the exterior of the original buildings were traditional, rustic log, the interiors were befitting an officer.

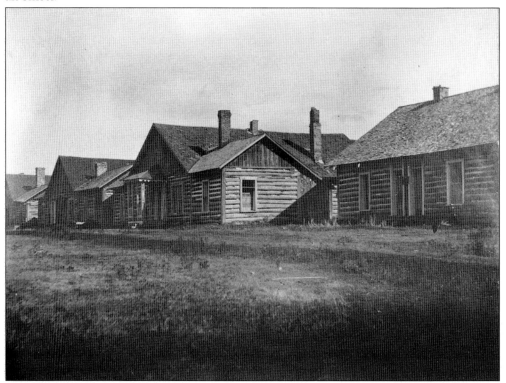

From 1867 until its closure in 1886, the officers' quarters at Fort Ellis were home to 65 officers. Notably, 13 of these officers were graduates of West Point.

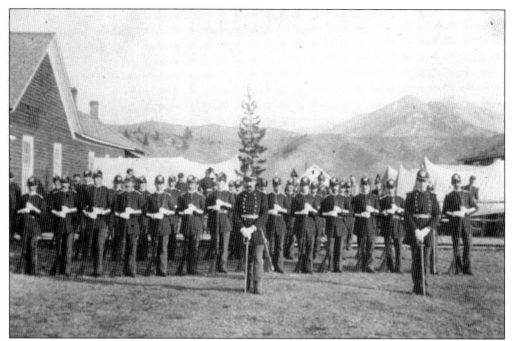

Fort Ellis was transferred to the Department of the Interior in July 1886, just one month before it was abandoned by the War Department. Later the Fort Ellis site was given to the State of Montana. It was used for Montana Militia Infantry practice. The Montana Militia Infantry is pictured in parade dress c. 1894.

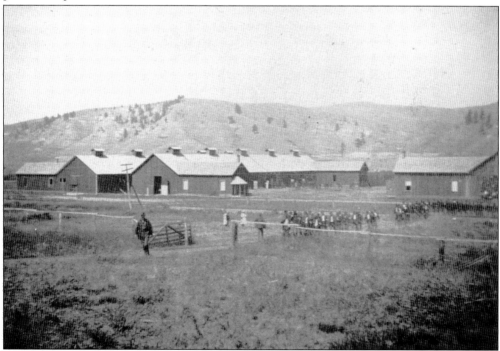

The Montana Militia conducted drills on the Fort Ellis grounds. Here the militia is pictured on the march some time during the 1890s.

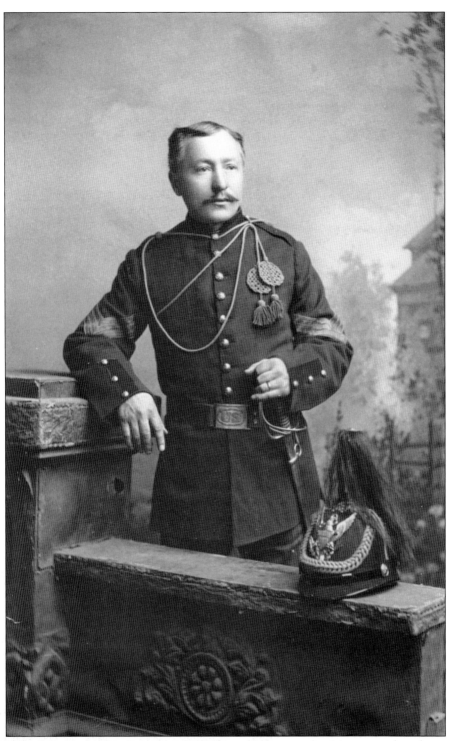

Rudolf Vogel Sr. was born in Switzerland in 1851 and later moved to Montana, where he opened the popular Tivoli Hotel and Saloon in Bozeman. Vogel, pictured in uniform, was a volunteer at the fort.

Three

BLACK GOLD
COAL FUELS THE ECONOMY

Col. James D. Chesnut opened
Montana's first commercial coal
mine just west of the Bozeman
Pass in 1867. The town of
Chesnut, later called Chestnut
after a postal clerk added a
T, soon sprang up. Chesnut
grew rich on coal exploration,
an endeavor others deemed
foolish. Although the coal
fields near Bozeman presented
many difficulties, the coal was
of excellent quality. It also had
the advantage of being located
near a military post and the
growing city of Bozeman.

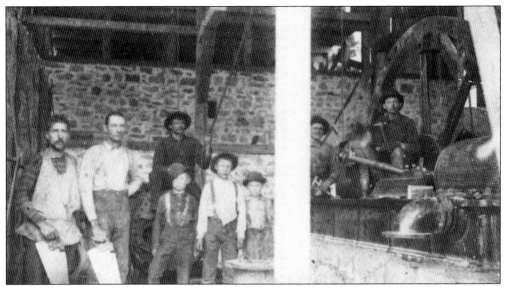

English born William Henry Williams built the first coke oven west of the Mississippi near Bozeman in 1882. Since coal did not burn hot enough to be an effective chemical reducing agent to change the state of metal ore, the process of making coke was critical to financial success. After Williams proved that the local coal deposits could be baked into coke, which burns hot enough to smelt metal, the heyday of the coal mining boom began in the area. By 1890, Cokedale had over 100 ovens.

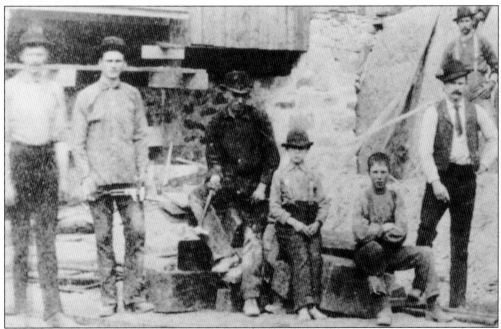

William Henry Williams, pictured second from the left, played an influential role in local coal production. Coal was key to the early development of the Gallatin Valley and also played an important role in the southern railway route. After a town sprang up near Cokedale, the Northern Pacific Railroad built a spur line to the town to create a more efficient route for getting the ore to market.

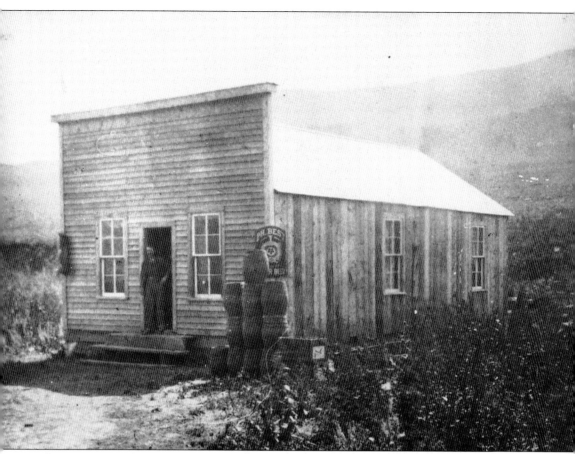

William Henry Williams also ran the Cokedale saloon in 1887. Each mining town had a unique personality and attracted immigrants from around the world. These colorful, rough-and-tumble residents helped make many Montana fortunes.

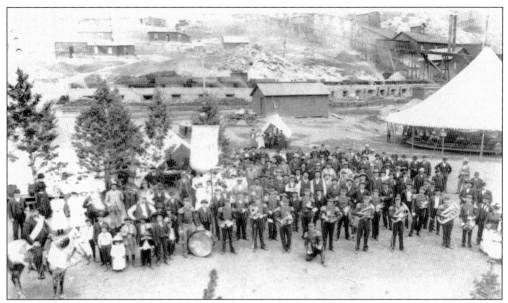

The busy miners of Cokedale took a day off for recreation with townspeople to celebrate on July 4, 1892. A carnival merry-go-round was set up for the children, and the Cokedale band performed. The coke ovens, which processed hundreds of tons of coal per day during Cokedale's boom years, are visible in the photograph.

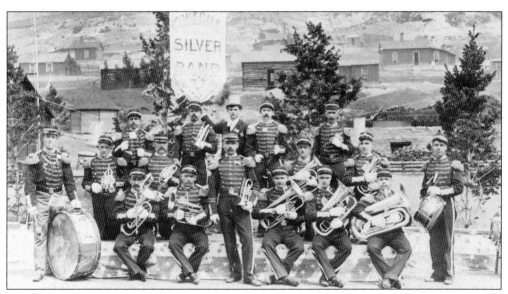

The Cokedale Silver Cornet Band, comprised mostly of local miners, proudly represented the region in performances around the state. Despite the low wages paid to miners, the members of the cornet band diligently raised money to outfit members in full dress regalia. Local lore suggests that community members thought the band would be therapeutic for its members by purging coal dust from their lungs by playing the instruments.

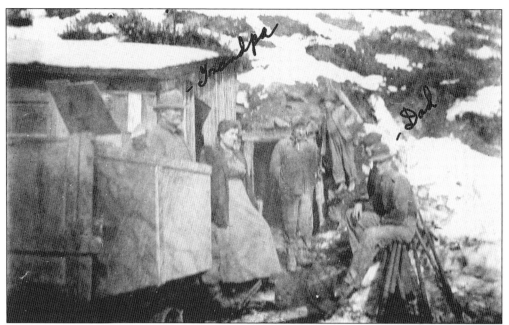

Henry and Charlie Cramer and others work a surface ledge near the Trevitick Mine. Coal mining was dirty and backbreaking work. From the late 1880s to the early 1900s, the coal camps were lively communities with a seemingly bright future. For a time, Bozeman supplied coke to nearby Butte for the copper industry. When the copper industry found a less expensive way to smelt its ore and bought less coal, the mining towns began their decline.

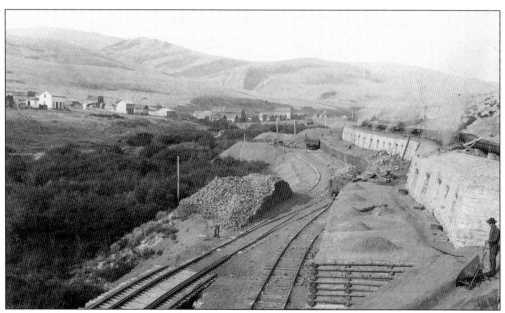

Coke ovens at the town of Cokedale transformed 200 tons of coal into 100 tons of coke each day. Coke is a solid material derived from the distillation of coal. The coal is baked in an airless oven at extremely high temperatures, where the ash and carbon are fused together. Coke burns at a high temperature with little or no smoke, making it useful for industrial applications.

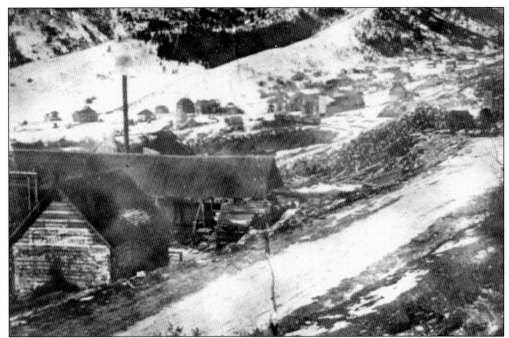

Colonel Chesnut's boundless enthusiasm and undaunted faith in the usefulness of coal led to his economic success. Although mining was difficult because the seams of coal were thin or broken in many places because of faulting, Chesnut held steadfast in his beliefs. The town of Chesnut, c. 1898, steadily grew along with the demand for coal.

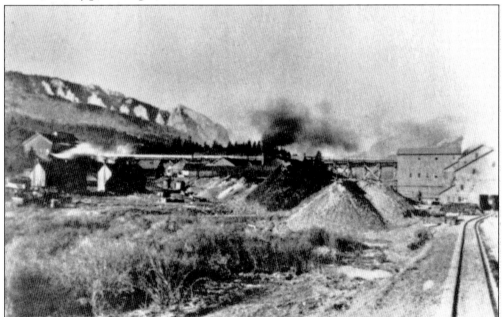

A 10-mile railroad spur line, dubbed the "Turkey Trail," ran through Chesnut c. 1904, as well as through other mining towns along Trail Creek Divide. Since it was now easier and less costly to transport coal to Bozeman and surrounding towns, coal became a more desirable and economically efficient fuel for home and business owners.

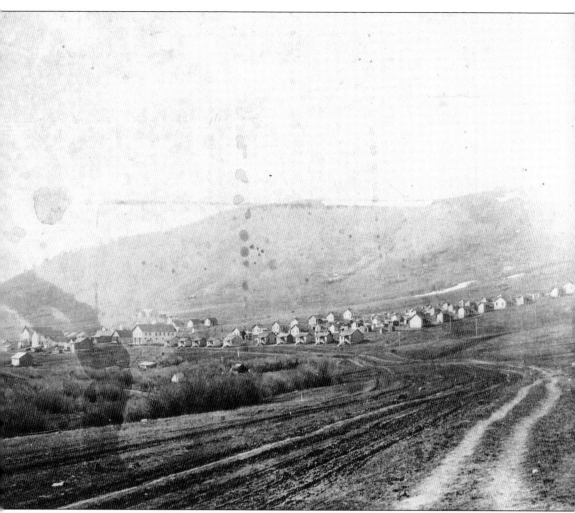

The town of Storrs, c. 1903, had about 1,000 residents and was billed as a "modern mining town." Neat rows of company houses with electric lights and running water made for comfortable living. Storrs was named for Lucius Storrs, a railroad geologist. The town of Storrs had a general store owned by the mining company, a boardinghouse, and a school. Some mining towns, such as Storrs, prohibited saloons in town, but resourceful entrepreneurs built saloons within walking distance of Storrs, which the locals dubbed "Whiskey Point." Storrs was abandoned in 1908.

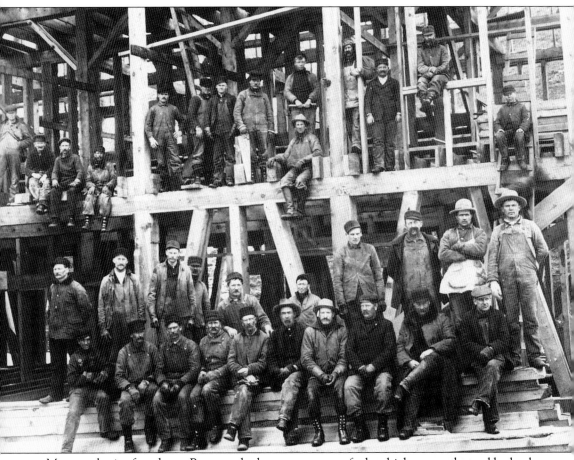

Many coal veins found near Bozeman had a great amount of ash, which meant the coal had to be prepared by washing it to ready it for sale or coking. Employees of the North Western Improvement Coal Washes (*c.* 1904), near Storrs, used wood-timbered washers to ready the coal for market. A costly venture, the coal washers could cost as much as $100,000 to build. This coal washer had to be rebuilt after it burned in 1904.

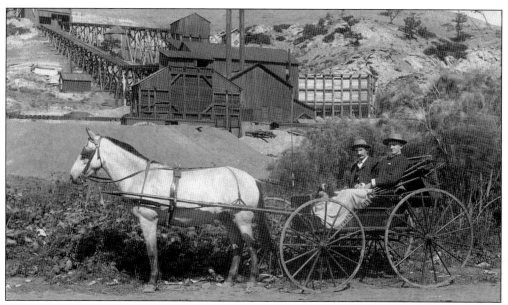

The buildings at the Cokedale mine sat above the underground operations. The mine shafts went 300 feet or more below the surface, where underground rooms were created. The rooms were braced with log pillars. After the miners dislodged chunks of coal from the veins, mules and horses pulled the coal to the surface for processing.

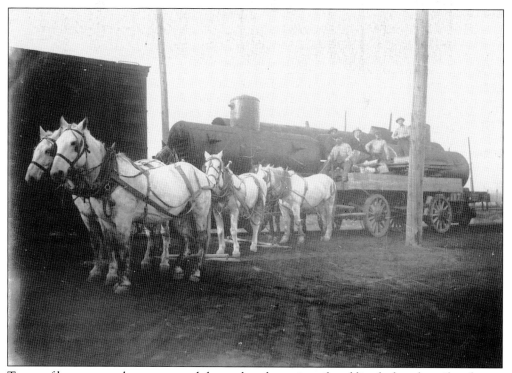

Teams of horses or mules transported the coal to the main railroad line before the railroad spurs reached the mining towns.

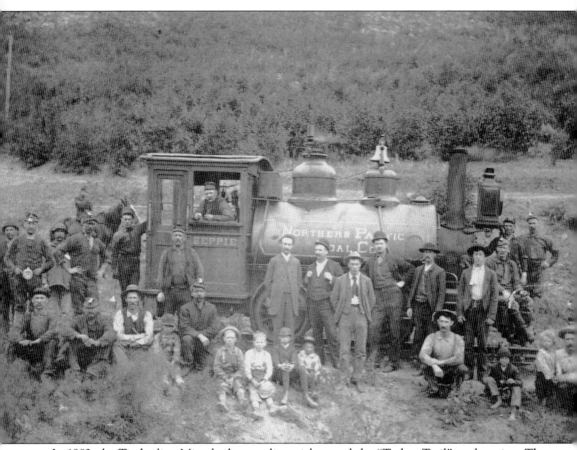

In 1882, the Timberline Mine had a spur line nicknamed the "Turkey Trail" to the mine. The spur lines streamlined the transportation of coal to market and made it a more profitable venture. The spur ran from Chesnut to Storrs and to the mines along Trail Creek. The locomotive, called "Heppie," simplified getting coal to the Northern Pacific mainline.

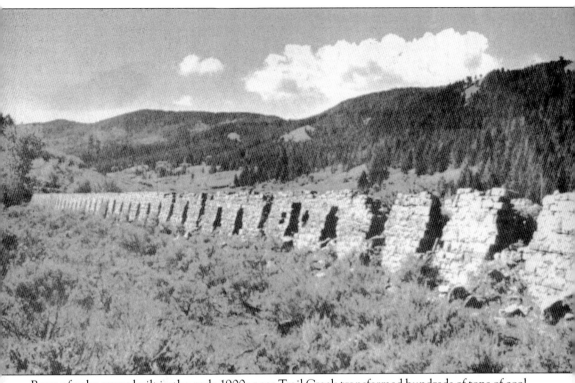

Rows of coke ovens built in the early 1900s near Trail Creek transformed hundreds of tons of coal per day. The gases, fluids, and impurities that rose into the air produced eye-burning gases every day. Mining operations in the Rockies caused a variety of negative environmental impacts.

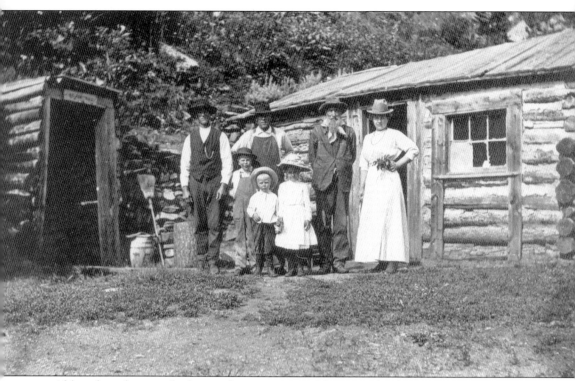

Although coal mining had a significant impact on Montana's development and economy, it was gold that started the mining boom. After gold was discovered at Virginia City and Alder Gulch around the time of the Civil War, the gold rush in Montana was on. But prospectors continued to come long after the initial gold rush. A prospector's family near Springhill still searched for gold in 1912. The entrance to the gold mine (at left) is next to the family's cabin.

Four

RIDING THE RAIL
SOUTHWARD

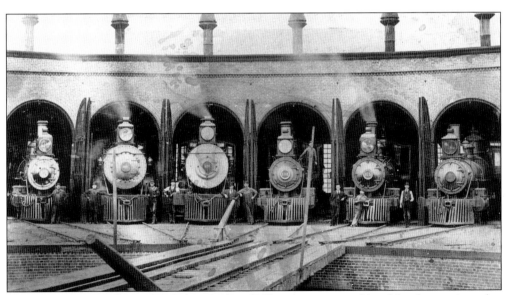

The Bozeman Roundhouse bustled in the late 1880s, when state and local freight terminated at the location. But the Northern Pacific Railroad moved the operations center west to the town of Logan around 1895, a decision that altered the course of both towns. The Bozeman Roundhouse was destroyed by fire in the late 1940s.

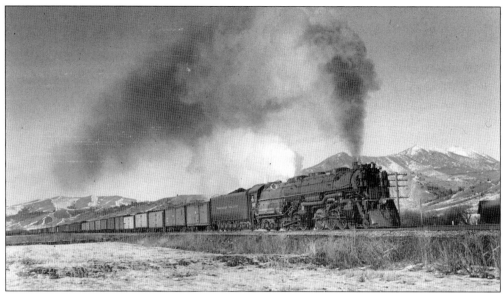

In 1883, the Northern Pacific Railroad made its first appearance in the Gallatin Valley. Although originally slated for a route through Northern Montana, the discovery of gold in Southwestern Montana and the vigorous lobbying efforts of local businessmen influenced the decision to bring the railroad through Bozeman Pass. A tunnel was completed to make the steep grade less dangerous. When the tunnel was completed in 1884, the railroad ran from Lake Superior in Minnesota to Puget Sound in Washington.

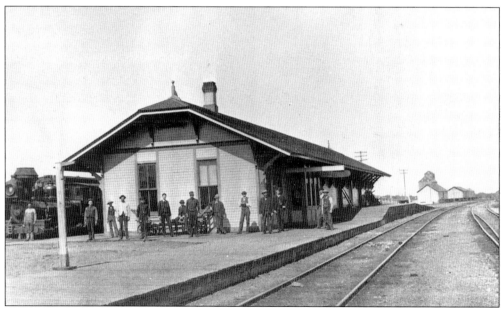

Bozeman's first depot opened in 1883 and was located about three-quarters of a mile away from town on Ida Avenue near the McAdow Flour Mill. The mill had donated 16 acres of land for the station, and the trains carried passengers and goods. A brick building replaced the wooden depot in 1891 after the original structure burned.

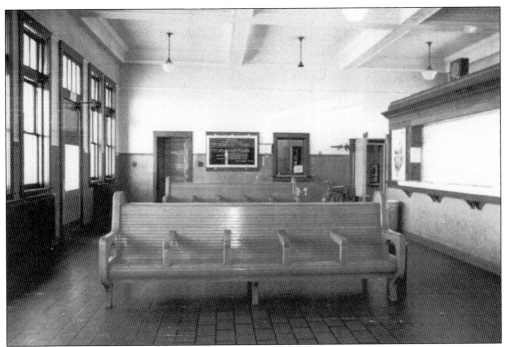

The interior of Bozeman's Northern Pacific Depot provided a comfortable and modern area for waiting passengers. When the railroad first arrived in Bozeman in March 1883, residents planned to commemorate the arrival. On that day, the town planned a parade to the new depot led by an infantry band from Fort Ellis with speeches planned by city and railroad officials. However, the parade to the tracks was abandoned because of impassable mud in the streets. The wagon that tried in vain to lead the way sunk up to its axles in the mud.

NORTHERN PACIFIC RAILROAD.

MONTANA DIVISION
AND BRANCHES.

No. 25 | TIME SCHEDULE | No. 25

TO TAKE EFFECT AT 11:59 P. M.

(MOUNTAIN OR 105th MERIDIAN TIME.)

(One hour slower than Central or 90th Meridian Time.)

SUNDAY, JUNE 4th, 1893.

SUCCEEDING CARDS AS SHOWN WITHIN.

For the government of employes only. The Company reserves the right to vary therefrom at pleasure. Be positive that you have the current card, and destroy all previous numbers. Read carefully the Special Rules, and always have for reference a copy of the TRANSPORTATION RULES.

M. C. KIMBERLY,
Gen'l Superintendent,

W. S. MELLEN,
Gen'l Manager.

G. W. DICKINSON,
Ass't Gen'l Superintendent.

T. J. DeLAMERE,

The Northern Pacific Railroad from 1893 gave passengers up-to-the-minute time schedules.

West Bound. Mountain or 105th Meridian Time, One Hour slower than Central or 90th Meridian Time.

TTE FREIGHT No. 59	WAY FREIGHT No. 57	FREIGHT No. 55	EXPRESS FR'T No. 53	Water, Coal, Tables and Wyes	Station Numbers	Time Card No. 25 June 4th, 1893 Succeeding No. 24A STATIONS	Distance from Livingston	PACIFIC MAIL No. 1	PACIFIC EX. Via Butte No. 3	PACIFIC EX. Via Helena No. 5	BUTTE PASS. Pacific Mail Connection No. 7
Third Class	Third Class	Third Class	Second Class					First Class	First Class	First Class	First Class
DAILY	DAILY	DAILY	DAILY					DAILY	DAILY	DAILY	DAILY
9.00 P M M 56	De 5.00 A M	De 11.15 A M	De 7.45 P M	WCTSY	1071	Livingston 4.6	0.0 De 5.25 ‖ ‖ 58	D+ 9.10 A M			
9.30 M 60	5.25	11.40 A M	8.10 M 56		1076	Coal Spur 4.4	4.6	5.35	F 9.30		
10.00	5.50	12.05 P M	8.35	W	1080	Hoppers 3.1	9.0	5.48	F 9.38		
10.20	6.10	12.25	8.50 M 60		1083	Muir 1.2	12.1	6.00 M 4	F 9.43		
10.30	6.20	12.35	9.00		1084	West End 0.6	13.3	6.06	F 9.51		
10.35	6.30	12.40	9.04		1085	Timber Line 1.9	13.9	6.08	F 9.53		
10.45	6.40	12.50	9.15		1087	Mountain Side 1.2	15.8	6.14	F 9.59		
10.50	6.50	12.56	9.20		1088	Chestnut 3.1	17.0	6.17	F 10.02		
11.05	7.05	1.12	9.33		1092	Gordon 4.7	20.1	6.24 M 56	F 10.09		
11.30 Ar 7.30 11.40 ‖ ‖ 54 De 8.00		Ar 1.35 M 53 De 1.45 M 8	Ar 9.55 De 10.00	WCST	1096	Bozeman 4.6	24.8 Ar 6.35 De 6.40	Ar 10.20 F 10.25	De 10.40 A M	De 6.55 P M
12.01 A M	8.30	2.10	10.23		1101	Storey 5.1	29.4	6.48 M 60	F 10.35	F 10.50	F 7.02 M 60
12.21	9.00	2.35	10.45 M 54		1106	Belgrade 5.5	34.5	6.57	F 10.46	F 11.01	F 7.12
12.45	9.25	3.00	11.10	W	1111	Central Park 3.9	40.0	7.07	F 10.57	F 11.12	F 7.22
1.02	9.45	3.20 M 56	11.25		1115	Manhattan 5.4	43.9	7.15	F 11.05	F 11.20	F 7.30
1.25 A M M 2 DAILY	10.15	Ar 3.45 De 3.50 M 6 & 4	11.45 P M	W C	1120	Logan 4.0	49.3	7.25	Ar 11.15 ‖ ‖ 58 DAILY	11.30 M 58	Ar 7.40 P M
or Page 5	10.35 M 58	4.05	12.05 A M	Y	1125	Gallatin 10.2	53.3	7.33	See Page 5	F 11.40	See Page 5.
	11.20	4.45	12.55		1135	Magpie 7.4	63.5	7.53		F 11.59 A M	
	11.50 A M	5.14	Ar 12.55 De 1.00 M 2	W	1142	Painted Rock 7.9	70.9	8.08 M 54		F 12.15 P M	
	Ar 12.27 P M 5 P De 12.37 M 56	5.45	1.27		1150	Toston 10.9	78.8	8.25		F 12.32 ‖ 56 ‖ 57	
	Ar 1.55 De 2.00 M 6	Ar 6.30 De 6.35 M 54	1.55	WCY	1161	Townsend 3.1	89.7	F 8.45		F 12.55	
B. V. & R. and E. & J. C.	2.25	6.50	2.35		1164	Bedford 5.4	92.8	8.53		F 1.03	
FREIGHT No. 61	2.45	7.15	3.15		1170	Vose 5.0	98.2	9.09		F 1.15	HELENA ACCN. No. 9
Third Class	3.25	7.35	3.35		1175	Winston 8.8	103.2	9.22		F 1.25 M 6	Second Class
DAILY		8.20	4.10		1183	Clasoil 6.6	112.0	9.38		F 1.43	DAILY
4.35 P M M 54	Ar 4.30 M 54 9 P De 5.05	9.00	4.35	S Y	1189	Prickley Pear Junc. 4.5	118.6	9.50		1.55	De 5.00 P M P M 54
4.55 P M	Ar 5.25 P M	Ar 9.30 P M	Ar 5.00 ‖ ‖ 58	WCSTY	1194	Helena	123.1 Ar 10.00 P M		Ar 2.05 P M	Ar 5.15 P M
DAILY	DAILY	DAILY	DAILY					DAILY		DAILY	DAILY

M—Meet. P—Pass. *—Trains do not stop for passengers. F—Flag Station. W—Water. C—Coal. S—Scale. T—Table. Y—Wye.
☞ Study Carefully Special and General Rules. Important changes have been made which must be understood alike by all.

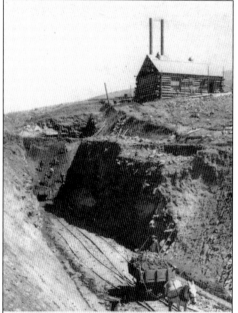

THIS PHOTOGRAPH SHOWS THE WESTERN APPROACH TO THE FIRST BOZEMAN TUNNEL DURING CONSTRUCTION IN 1882 AND THE NEARLY-COMPLETED PUMPING STATION WHICH DREW WATER FROM MIDDLE CREEK OVER BOZEMAN PASS FOR GROUND-SLUICING OF THE EASTERN APPROACH. WHEN COMPLETED, THE TRACKS IN THIS TUNNEL HAD A MAXIMUM ELEVATION ABOVE SEA-LEVEL, O 5,562 FEET - HIGHEST POINT ON THE NORTHERN PACIFIC RAILROAD FROM LAKE SUPERIOR TO PUGET SOUND. (F. J. HAYNES PHOTO, AUGUST, 1882.)

This Northern Pacific Railroad schedule gave the pick-up times for stations such as Hoppers, Magpie, and Prickley Pear Junction.

In the fall of 1881, work began on the tunnel through Bozeman Pass. By December 1883, daylight was visible through both ends of the tunnel. Much of the difficult and tedious work was performed by Chinese laborers. Large mudslides of wet clay slowed the process. The tunnel was finally completed in January 1884, and the first freight train passed through on January 19, 1884. The first tunnel, lined with brick and concrete, was 16 feet wide and 1,919.75 feet high and 3,652 feet long. A fire and cave-in closed the tunnel for nearly a year in September 1895.

Workers faced great challenges placing railroad track over the Bozeman Pass. The cost of this engineering feat was unprecedented in scope. Rocky terrain and steep grades presented obstacles at every turn. Grading was done by hand with horse-drawn tools and dynamite.

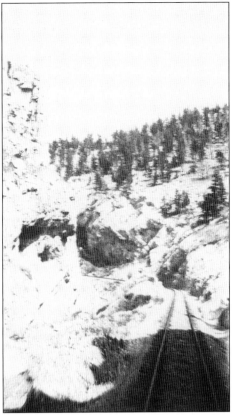

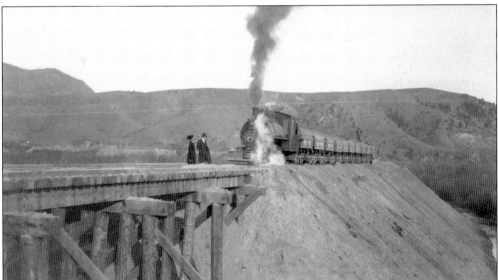

Isaac Stevens had recommended a route for the railroad passing through Montana be around 200 miles north of Bozeman following the Missouri and Milk River Valleys. The southern route may have been chosen because of the mining development in the southwest, the military posts and the Indian Agencies, but most likely it was due to the vigorous lobbying efforts of Bozeman businessmen.

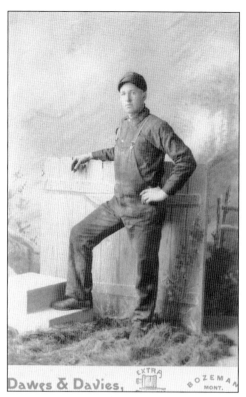

Dawes & Davies, BOZEMAN MONT.

Railroad work was a tough and dangerous business in the late 1880s in Montana. Switchmen were required to jump between cars and connect heavy couplings, which was especially dangerous work. Brakemen had to jump between car roofs to turn the brake wheels. LeRoy Homer Mercer, an experienced engineer, took the position of wiper at the request of his wife because she thought it would be safer. However, Mercer met his untimely demise in 1899 when he was crushed by an engine that jumped the track.

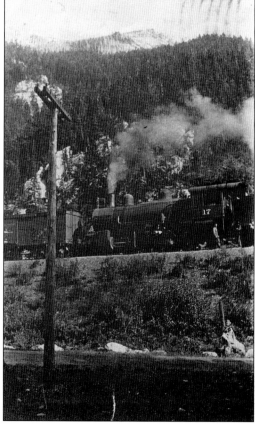

The railroad had a significant impact on the development of mining and agriculture and helped transform the state of Montana. The decade of the 1880s was the period of greatest growth and laid the foundations for statehood in 1889. Rail transportation, such as Engine No. 17, allowed the vast wealth of Montana resources to be marketable.

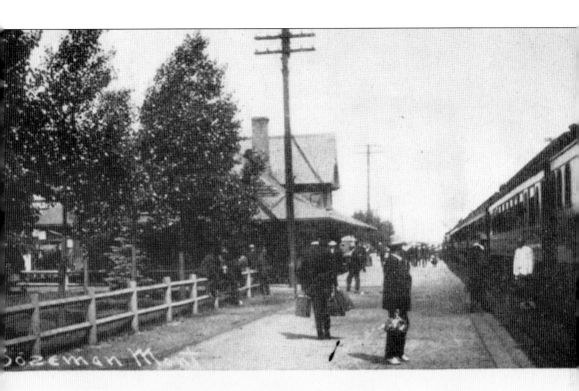

Railroad Station, Bozeman, Mont.

The Bozeman Passenger Depot, *c.* 1908, was updated after it was destroyed by fire in 1891. The busy depot greeted passengers coming from around the country.

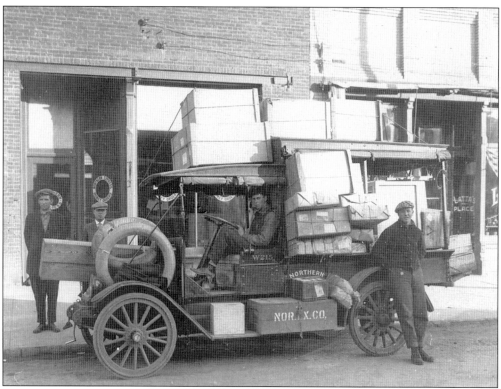

Northern Railway Express agent driver Frank Sexton, c. 1917, had the task of transporting goods that arrived via the railway to local businesses in downtown Bozeman. The railroad provided swift and low-cost transportation of goods, giving Bozeman consumers more choices at the marketplace.

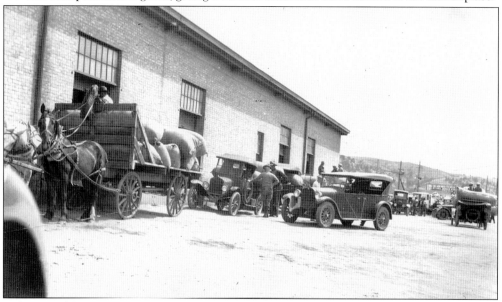

Picking up deliveries at the Bozeman Freight Depot, c. 1925, created an odd amalgam of horse-drawn wagons carrying sacks of wool and Model T open touring cars. The railroad greatly advanced the booming agricultural expansion of the Gallatin Valley.

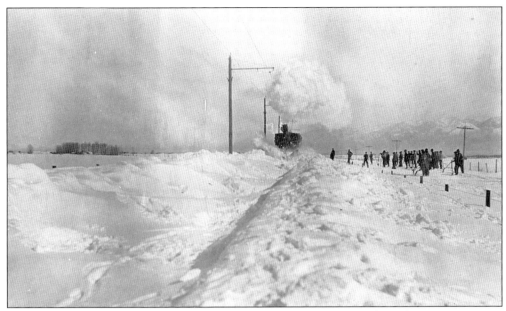

Harsh winters in Montana presented unique challenges for the railroad.

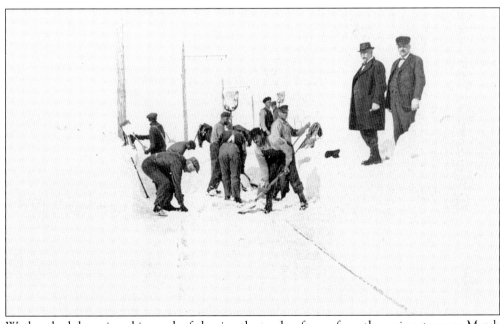

Workers had the painstaking task of clearing the tracks of snow from the spring storm on March 28, 1917, with shovels so the Gallatin Valley Railway train could continue its journey.

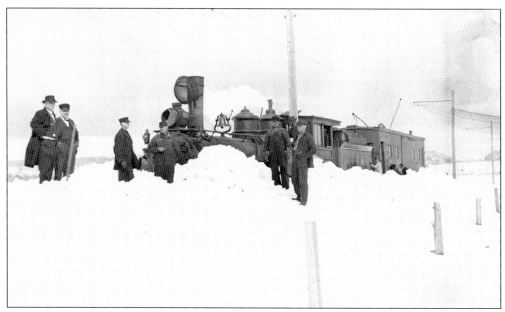

It was no small feat to clear the tracks to allow the train to reach Bozeman.

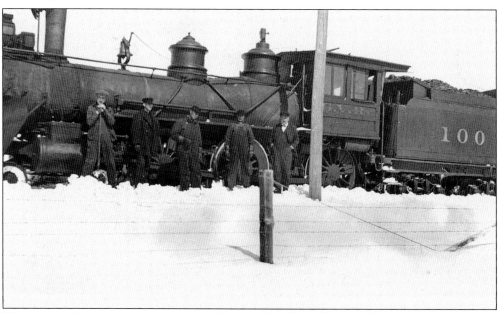

Unnamed workers pose with the engine that they freed from the snow bank.

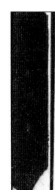

GALLATIN VALLEY RAILWAY.
(BOZEMAN STREET RAILWAY)

$1.00	20 RIDE BOOK.	$1.00

Form 20 B.   No. 6727

POOLE BROS. CHICAGO.

The Gallatin Valley Railway ride book gave passengers 20 rides for $1.

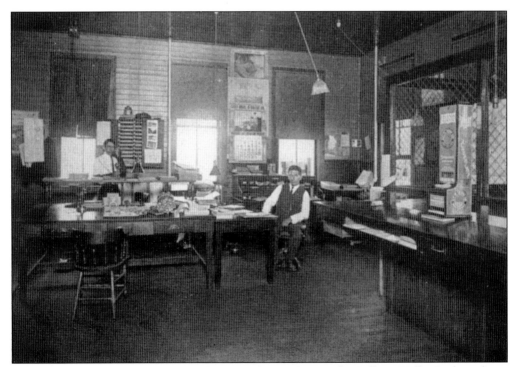

Passengers could purchase tickets for the interurban railway at the Gallatin Valley Railway depot on East Main Street in Bozeman.

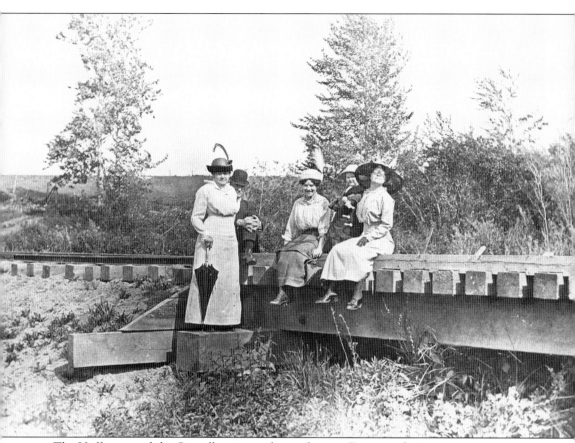

The Huffmans and the Orswells pose on the tracks near Bozeman during an outing.

Five

THE EGYPT OF AMERICA

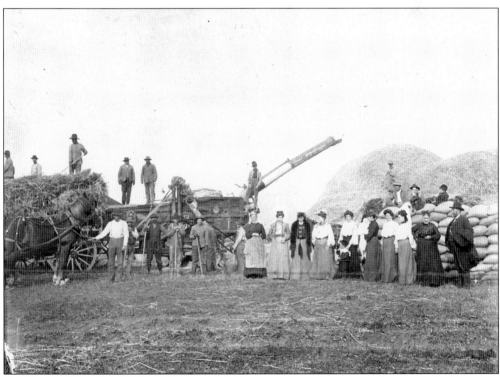

The fertile soil of the Gallatin Valley drew farmers and ranchers from the east. John Bozeman speculated that the area would ultimately become the "Garden of Montana" because of the rich land. The threshing machine, without a doubt, changed the face of agriculture near Bozeman. Prior to the introduction of the threshing machine, grain was separated from the stalks and husks by hand, a tiring and time-consuming task. The influx of grain kept the region's gristmills busy grinding over 320,000 sacks of flour weighing 98 pounds each.

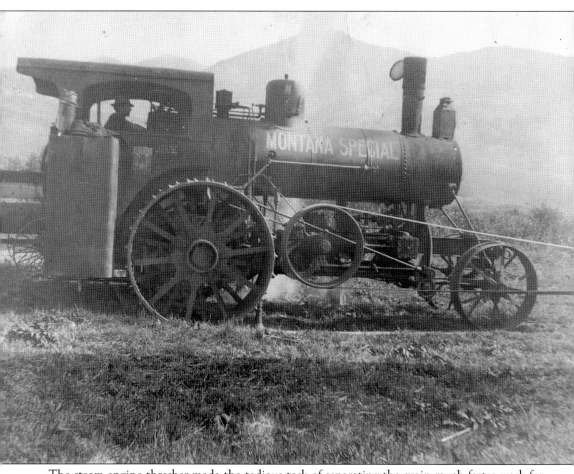

The steam engine thresher made the tedious task of separating the grain much faster work for crews. This engine was aptly named the *Montana Special.*

During harvest time, workers cut the stalks of grain and tied them in bundles; this was called grain shocking. Even after the advent of the threshing machine, some workers still performed the shocking by hand. John "Stubs" Staffanson, *c.* 1921, works in the field with others shocking the grain.

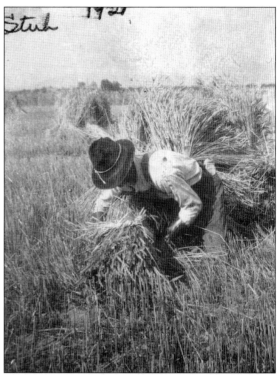

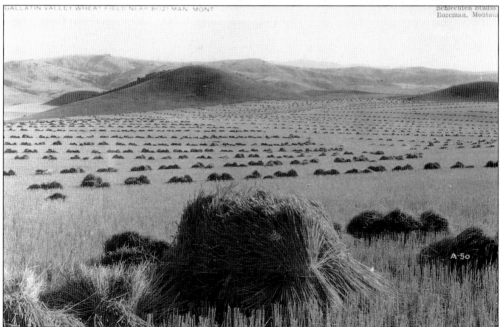

By 1911, Belgrade was a major wheat shipping center. Grain wagons lined up for 2 to 3 miles during harvest season. It was such a major task that in 1913, a railroad branch line was built northward from Bozeman to Menard. The 24.9-mile branch line was nicknamed the "Turkey Red Special" for the type of wheat that was imported from Turkey at the end of World War I. (Photograph by Schlechten Studios.)

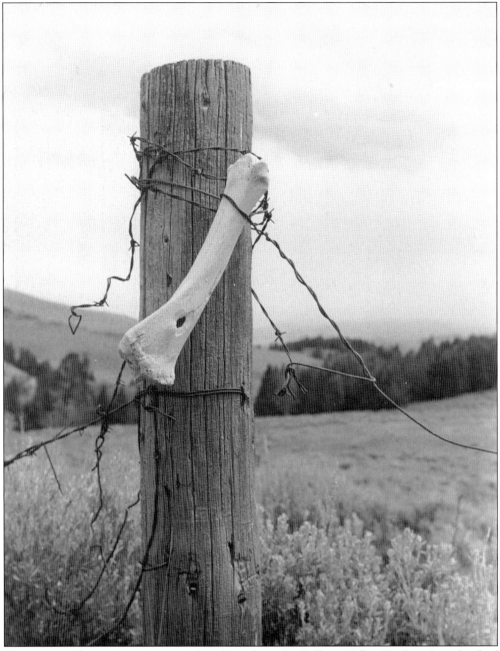

The resourceful pioneer spirit was evident throughout the Gallatin Valley. Tools and supplies had to make the long journey up the Missouri River, and not enough were available for all who needed them. Since farming tools were scarce, farmers and ranchers had to make do with materials they found at hand. An imaginative rancher used a dried bone as a fence tightener.

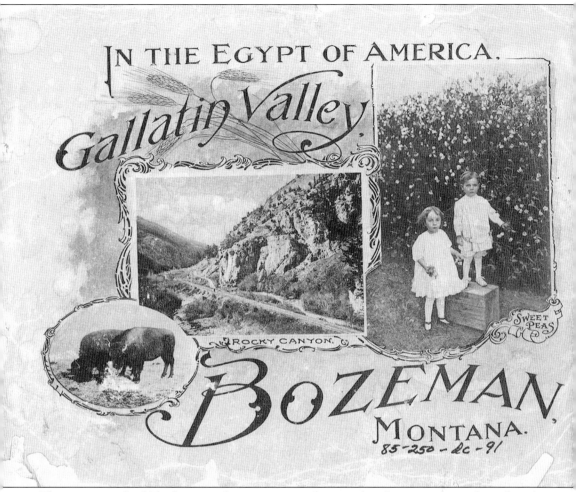

IN THE EGYPT OF AMERICA.

Gallatin Valley.

ROCKY CANYON.

SWEET PEAS

BOZEMAN, MONTANA.

85-250-2c-91

The prospect of gold had attracted newcomers to the area, but for many, it was the rich soil that made them stay. Creative farmers soon realized that someone needed to supply food for the growing population. Although farming on the high plains was far different from eastern conditions, farmers soon learned irrigation methods. As predicted, the region quickly became the "Egypt of America."

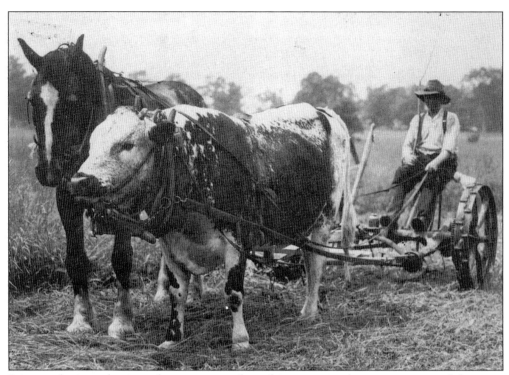

Prior to the introduction of steam-powered machinery, animal power was one of the most important resources. When a team of horses wasn't available, this innovative farmer did the next best thing—he used a cow.

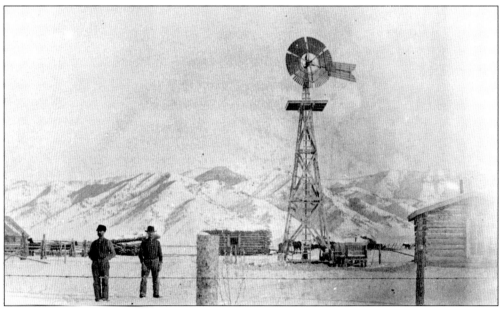

The 1880s saw a significant expansion in farming in Montana. In 1880, Montana had 1,519 farms. As the railroad entered the area, agriculture experienced a boom. By 1890, the number of farms skyrocketed to 5,603. These two unidentified men pose at the Buell Ranch.

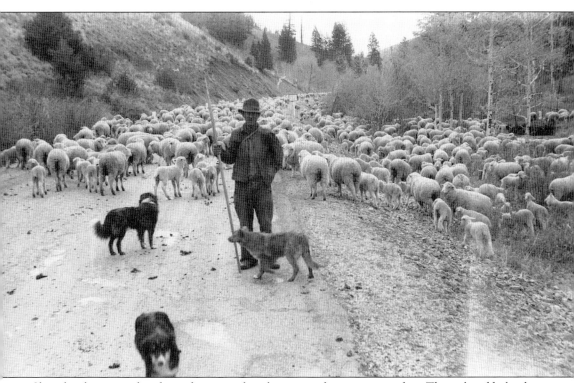

Sheepherding was a lonely profession with only canines for companionship. The railroad helped fuel the sheep and cattle boom of the region.

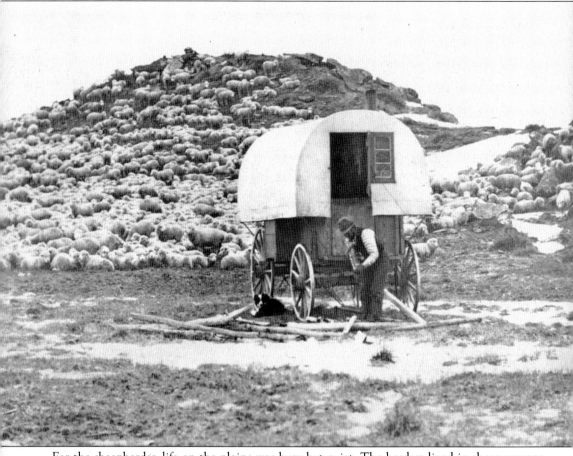

For the sheepherder, life on the plains was busy but quiet. The herders lived in sheep wagons, portable and compact living quarters that provided shelter in inclement weather. A predecessor to the modern-day travel trailer, these well-designed wagons had a heat source, a bed, and a place to cook. This shepherd is pictured around 1890. (Photograph by L. A. Huffman.)

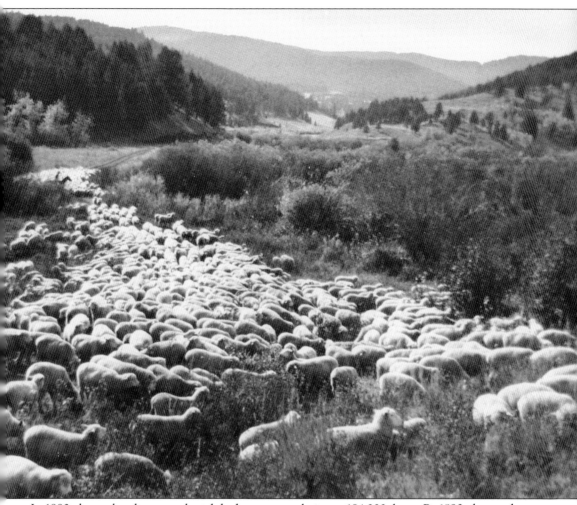

In 1880, sheep already outnumbered the human population at 184,000 sheep. By 1890, the number of sheep increased sharply to 1.8 million. Hundreds of sheep, pictured near Bozeman in Bridger Canyon, are herded up Skunk Creek.

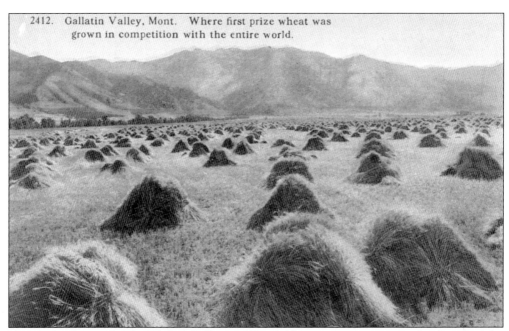

2412. Gallatin Valley, Mont. Where first prize wheat was grown in competition with the entire world.

Hundreds of grain shocks fill this Gallatin Valley field as a testament to the fertile soil of the region. In the mid-1860s, farmers in the valley harvested around 20,000 bushels of wheat. Near the end of the decade, that number increased to over 300,000 bushels.

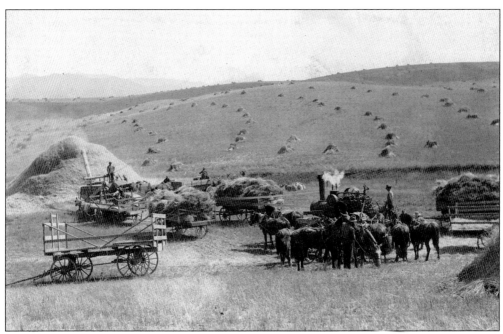

Threshing crews at the Alonzo Dwight Ranch, near Springhill, are pictured after a long day in the fields.

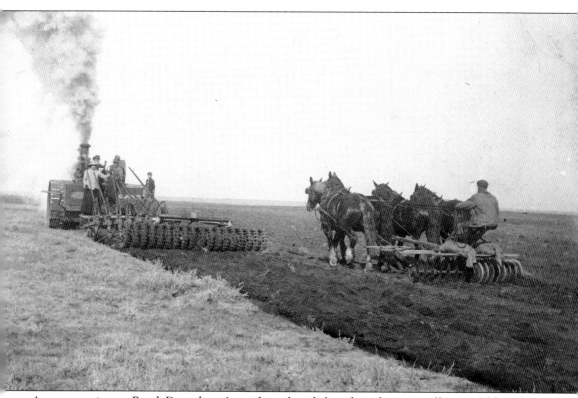

A steam engine on Brock Dusenberry's ranch works side by side with a team of horses. Although plows were typically pulled by teams of horses, the use of the wheeled steam engine revolutionized agriculture and dramatically increased productivity for local farms.

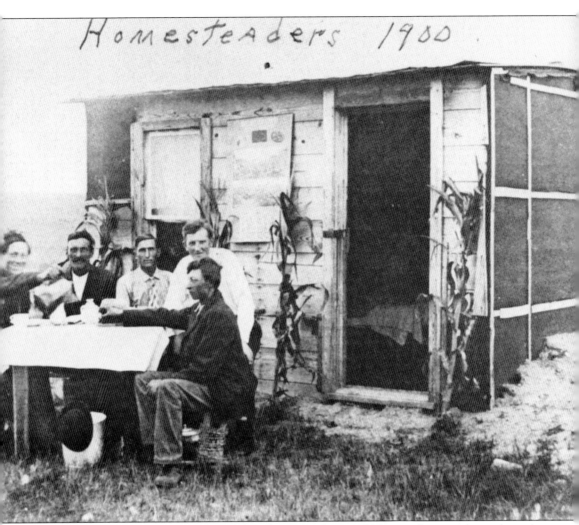

Although the names and stories of these homesteaders in 1900 are unknown, the pride in their living accommodations is apparent. Corn stalks are placed decoratively along the front of the simple cabin where the group prepares to share a meal.

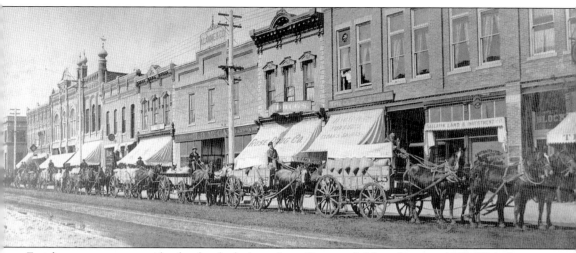

Freight wagons transport loads of sacked wheat down Bozeman's Main Street in 1905. With the exception of the onion domes (visible atop a building at left in the picture), which were toppled in an earthquake, many of the current buildings in downtown were originally built over 100 years ago.

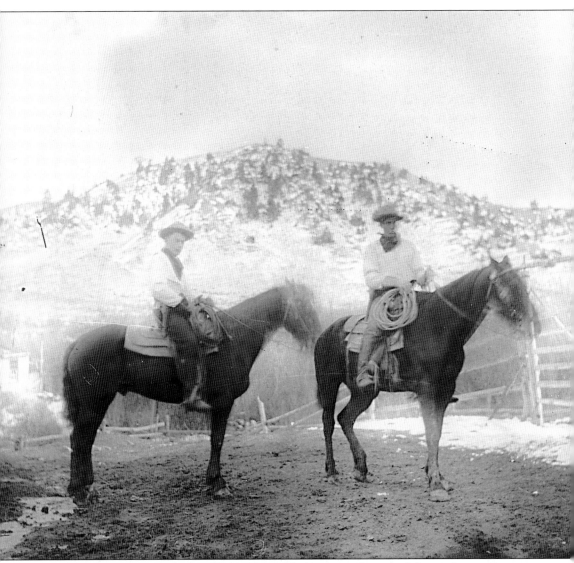

Where there are cows, there will be cowboys. The traditional image of the cowboy is synonymous with the West. These hardworking men rode the range keeping a watchful eye over a rancher's livestock. Popularized in rodeos, cowboys used their real-life skills of roping, lassoing, and tying in the course of their jobs.

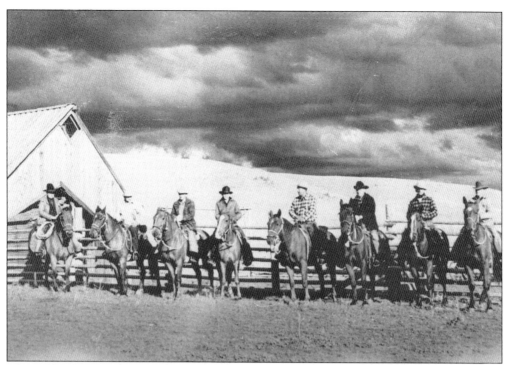

The railheads and the newly opened range land created a cattle and sheep boom. By 1880, Montana's ranges held slightly more than 160,000 head of cattle. By 1890, that number increased to over 667,000. These cowboys pose at the Flying D Ranch.

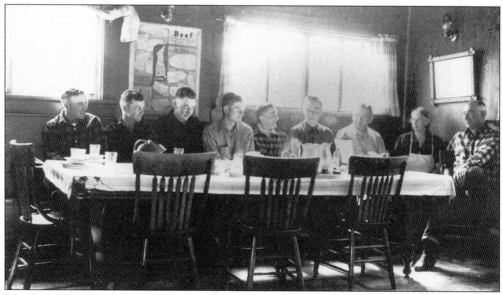

The dining room at the Flying D Ranch cow camp is pictured. Originally the Childs and Anceney Ranch, it later became the Flying D, which covered 120,000 acres or 25 square miles. Part of the acreage of the Flying D was purchased by Ted Turner in 1989. From left to right, Stanley Laird, Jim Pratt, Roy Laird, Bill Shunk, Grady Woirhay, Johnny Flowers, Larry McDonald, Mary Nerbovig, and Howard Lewis are pictured at camp c. 1946.

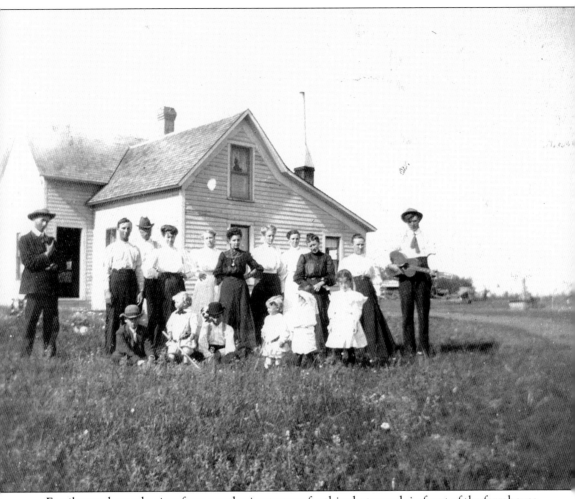

Family members take time from a gathering to pose for this photograph in front of the farmhouse. Although their names and stories are unknown, they symbolize the heart of the agricultural community of the Gallatin Valley.

Six

GETTING DOWN TO BUSINESS

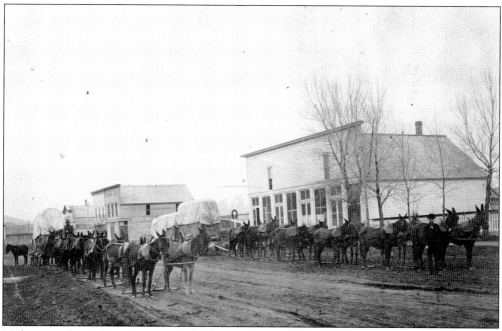

Mule trains line Main Street in early downtown Bozeman. Businessmen in Bozeman quickly realized that providing goods and services to the steady stream of immigrants would be a lucrative and profitable venture.

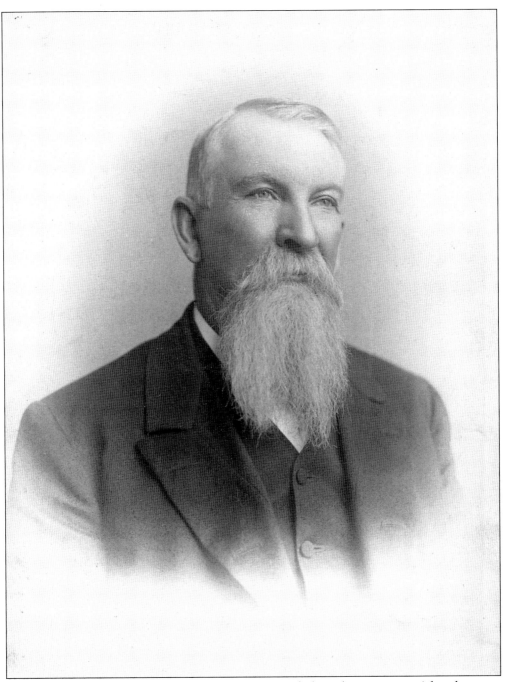

Originally from Ohio, Nelson Story was an eager and clever businessman. After driving a thousand longhorns from Texas to Montana, Story began to look for other ways to make money in Bozeman.

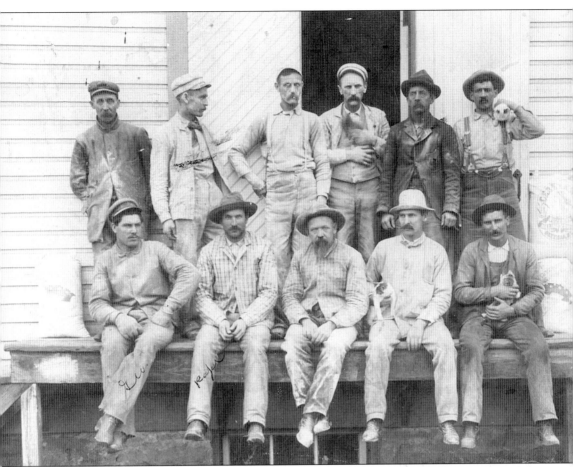

After Story bought the McAdow Flour Mill in the 1860s, he worked toward eliminating the competition by buying other mills and shutting them down. He later added a cereal mill on North Rouse Avenue. Workers at Bozeman's Story Cereal Mill are pictured with some of their feline friends. Story sold his profitable business to Montana Flour Mills in 1919. This mill operated for 83 more years.

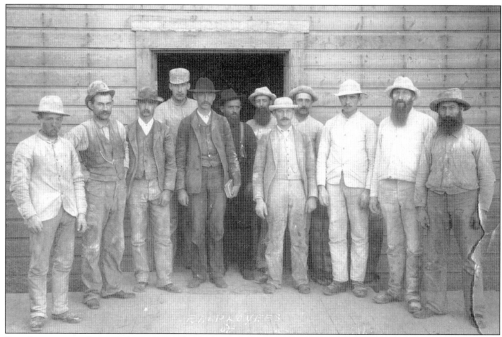

Employees standing in front of Nelson Story's flour mill in northeast Bozeman near the mouth of Bridger Canyon are pictured sometime before 1897. Built in 1882, Story claimed the mill was one of the largest daily producers of flour. The railroad soon built a spur line to the mill. Nelson Story's nephew, Elias Story Jr. (near the center, holding a book), was the manager of the mill.

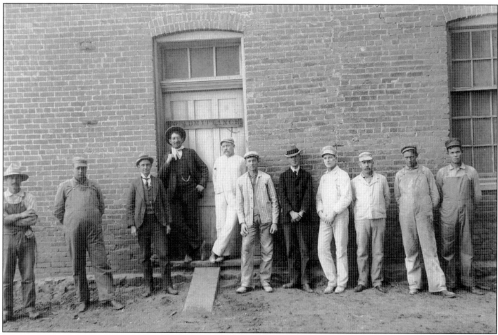

The railroad spur line led to the demise of the wooden Story Flour Mill in 1901. Sparks from a nearby train caused the mill to catch fire and burn to the ground. The mill was quickly rebuilt on the site, but brick was used the second time to prevent future disasters.

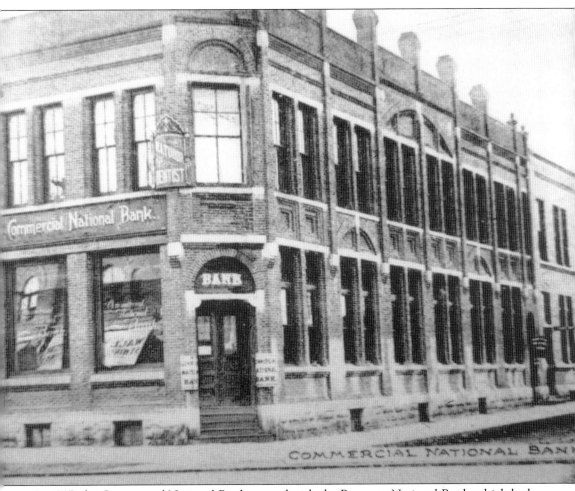

In 1907, the Commercial National Bank merged with the Bozeman National Bank, which had returned to prosperity after closing during a financial panic in 1893. The Commercial National Bank later became First Security Bank, which remains a well-known cornerstone of Bozeman's financial community.

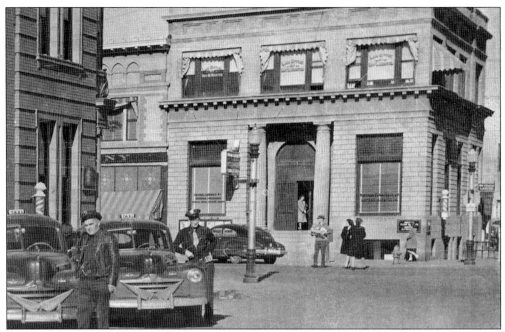

On August 29, 1872, the *Avant Courier* reported, "We think that the opening of this [the First National Bank of the Gallatin Valley] bank, at a time when our farmers are reaping and garnering unusually large crops, will be the commencement of an easier money market and better times." The First National Bank of the Gallatin Valley opened shortly thereafter in September 1872. The bank is pictured many decades later in a bustling downtown scene.

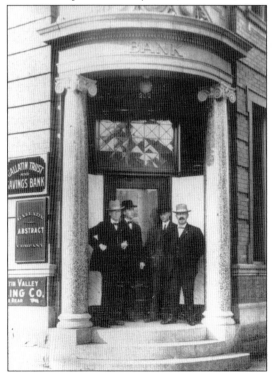

The Gallatin Trust and Savings Bank, originally the Gallatin State Bank, was established in 1902. The architecture conveys the feeling of prosperity in the early 20th century. Many of the buildings that line Main Street today were built between 1900 and 1910, illustrating that the city thrived during those years. The population of the city in 1900 was 3,450, and by 1910 there were 8,000 residents. W. S. Davidson is pictured at left.

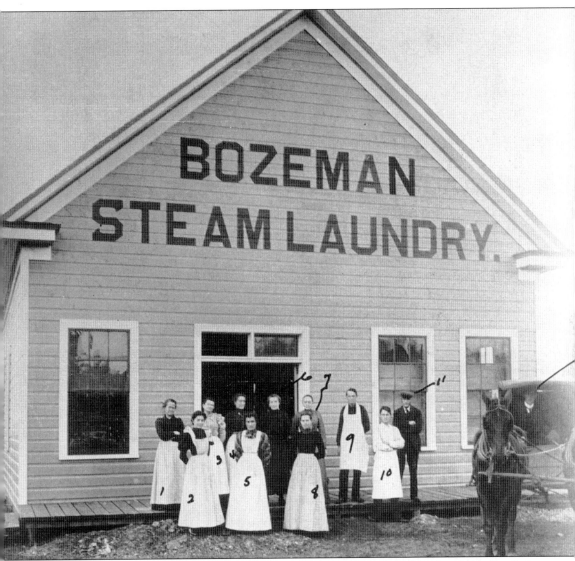

Mary Flora Kopp Haugen immigrated to the United States from Switzerland with her family in 1882. She later traveled to Bozeman via wagon. Mary Flora's husband, Josef, wanted to move farther west and took the family to Astoria, Oregon. But after Josef died in 1888, Mary Flora moved back to Bozeman with her eight children. After a few successful business ventures, she and partner Henry Topel opened the Bozeman Steam Laundry, which was the first in Montana. As the equipment arrived, Mary Flora found out that two of her employees were attempting to take over her new business. She fired them, but not before they could destroy some of the machinery. Mary Flora was able to restore the equipment and successfully opened her business. This business, now the Gallatin Laundry, still operates today. Mary Flora is identified in this photograph as No. 2.

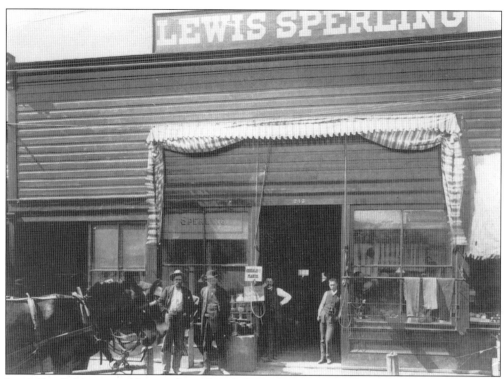
Lewis Sperling's store sold general merchandise on Main Street in the early 1880s.

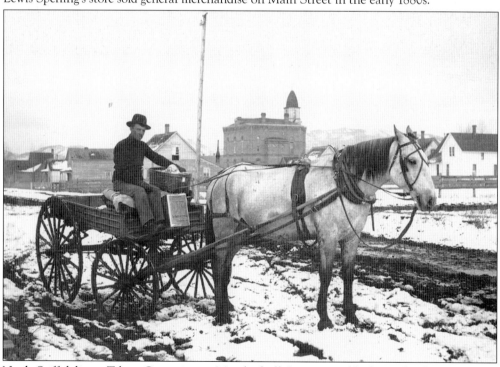
Noah Stiff delivers Tilton Groceries on Mendenhall Street, one block north of Main Street, c. 1900.

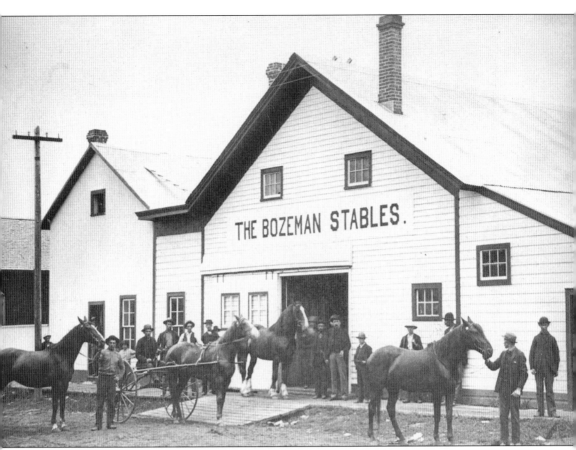

The Bozeman Stables served as the town's livery.

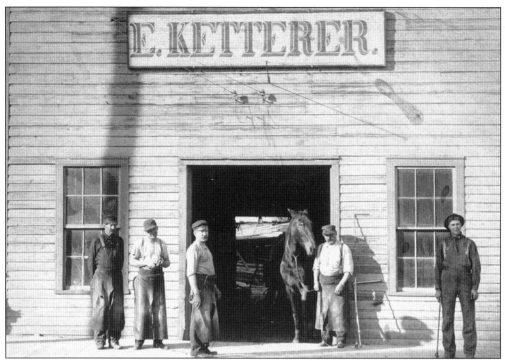

Emil Ketterer's Blacksmith Shop was located on the corner of Main Street and North Grand Avenue.

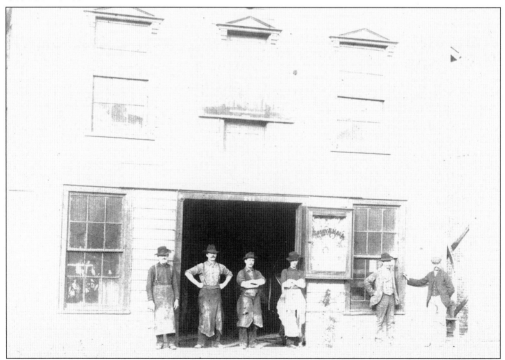

The business of the resourceful Busby and Hall featured a variety of miscellaneous services, including blacksmithing and sign painting.

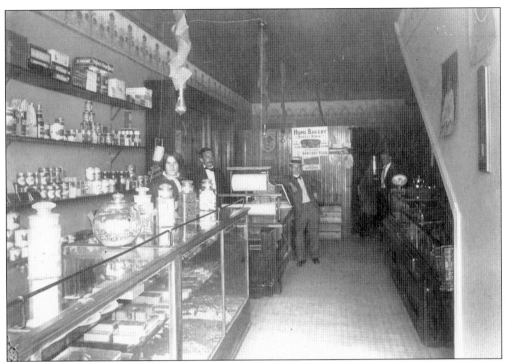

The interior of Home Bakery is pictured around 1914. Home Bakery was the predecessor to the popular Bon Ton Bakery, owned by Eugene Graf, which was located at the corner of Main Street and Willson Avenue. Although the building had several other incarnations, the Bon Ton sign remains on the facade.

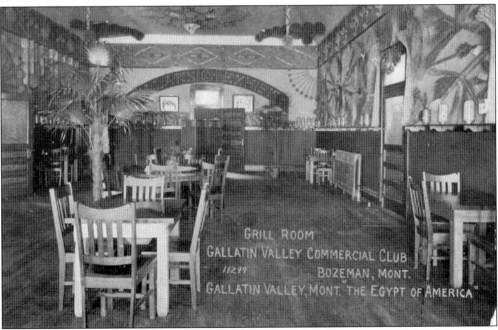

The Gallatin Valley Commercial Club was the local businessmen's group. The elegant Grill Room, located in the Bozeman Hotel, is pictured.

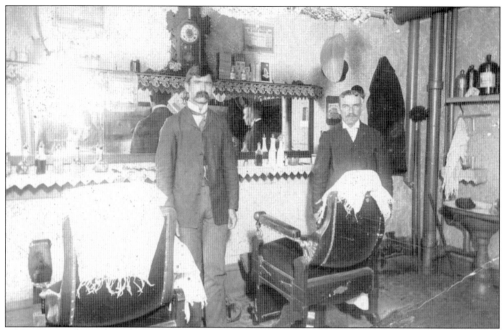

Barbers were an important part of downtown commerce. One of the most popular barbers was Samuel Lewis, an African American. He was known for many talents, including his musical abilities and the home he built at 209 South Tracy Avenue, which is on the National Historic Register. Unfortunately, no photograph exists of Lewis.

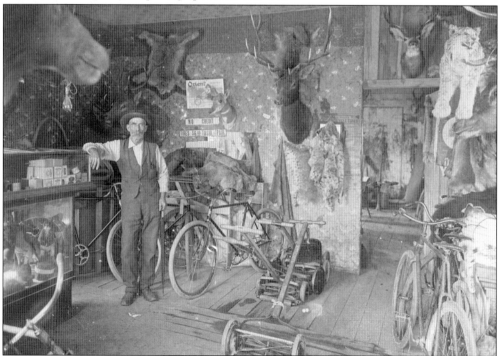

James Ginn, pictured in 1901, had a thriving bicycle shop on Main Street where the Ellen Theatre now stands.

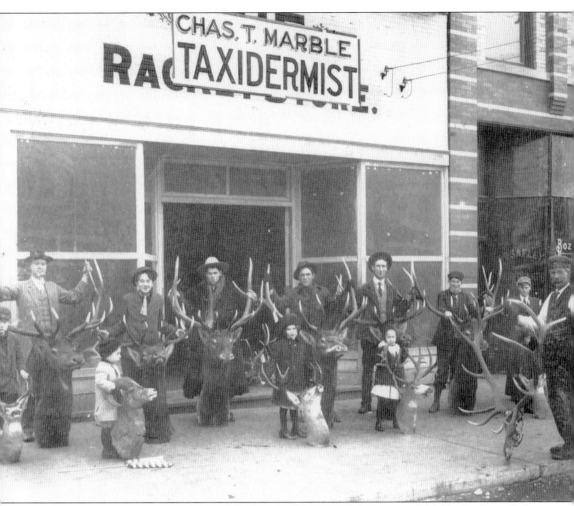

Charles Marble (pictured at right front) had a colorful past with his partner Dick Rock, also called "Rocky Mountain Dick." After years of working with Rock as a mountain guide and collector of wild animals, Marble left the wild life to open a taxidermy shop in downtown Bozeman. Rock was not so fortunate. He died after being gored by a supposedly tame buffalo.

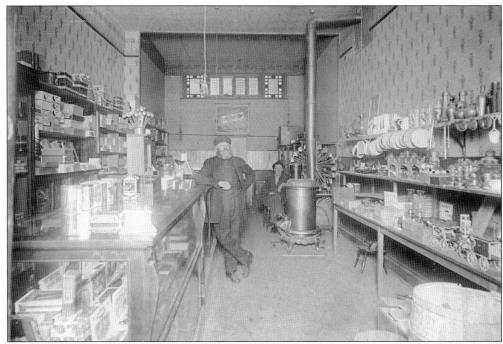

"Grandpa" Stuve manned the Stuve Store on Main Street. The store's shelves are stocked with an assortment of items needed by people in town. The original wooden building burned down and was replaced by a brick structure, which is now the location of MacKenzie River Pizza Company.

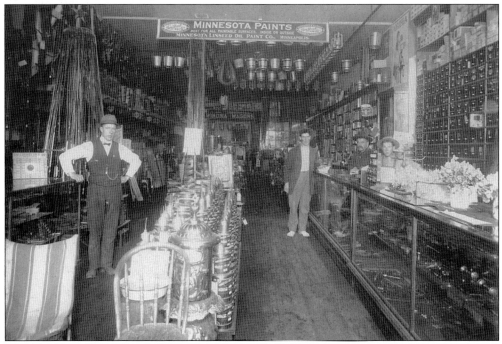

Henderson Hardware Store, *c.* 1915, sold everything from hardware to harnesses and from agricultural implements to fishing poles. Pictured are Claude Henderson, Pa Henderson, Will Henderson, and an unidentified customer.

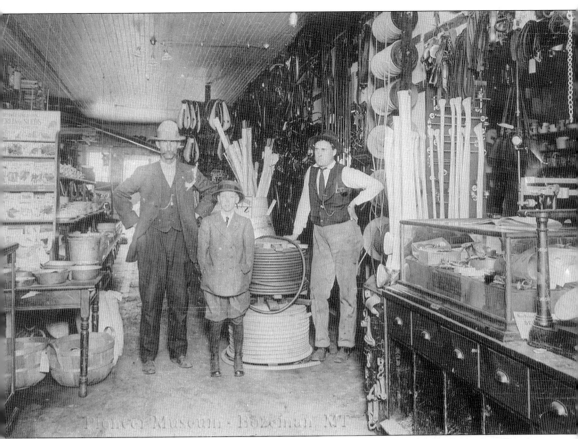

Felenzer's Hardware in Bozeman was one of the many hardware stores that sold an impressive and diverse array of goods for the growing town. John Bowles is pictured with Jim and store manager F. Harold Haskins. Another early downtown hardware store, Owenhouse Hardware, has been in operation for over 100 years and is still located in downtown Bozeman in 2008.

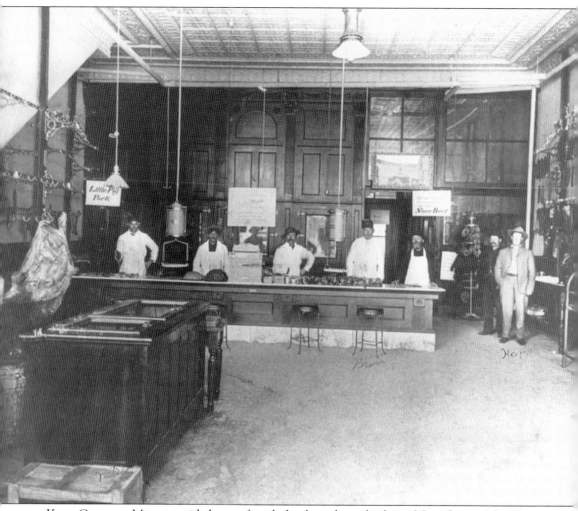

Kopp Company Meats provided meat for wholesale and retail sale on Main Street. John Kopp Jr. is pictured at right next to Louie Gross. Many members of the Kopp family, including Mary Flora Kopp, owner of the Bozeman Steam Laundry, arrived later.

As the town grew, businesses prospered in Bozeman. The Gallatin County Mercantile, located on Main Street, sold a variety of goods that residents of the growing town needed. Some early businesses prospered and still remain in business today, such as Phillip's Bookstore.

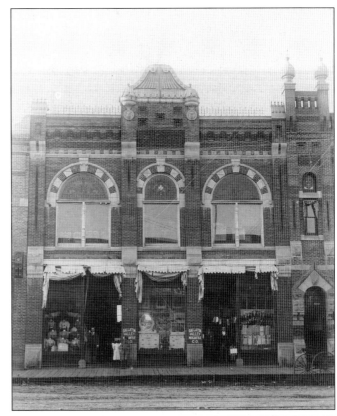

By 1888, Bozeman's downtown featured many examples of the grand architecture of the period. There are 49 buildings on the National Register of Historic Places in the Main Street Historic District, a clear testament to the elegant design of the early 1900s.

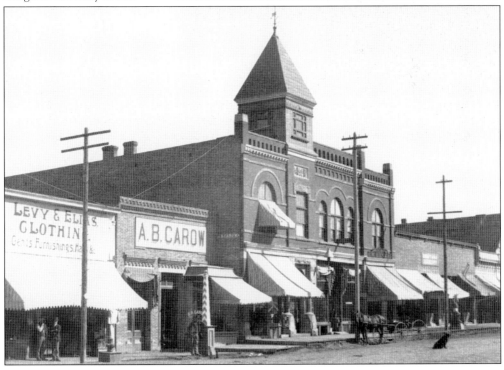

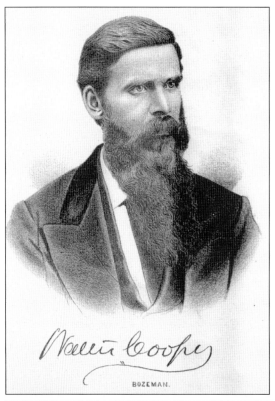

BOZEMAN.

Walter Cooper was a gunsmith and entrepreneur. He ran timber operations in Bear Canyon and Gallatin Canyon. The timber business supplied railroad ties for the growing railroad operations and mining timbers for nearby Butte. (Etching from Michael Leeson: *History of Montana*, 1885.)

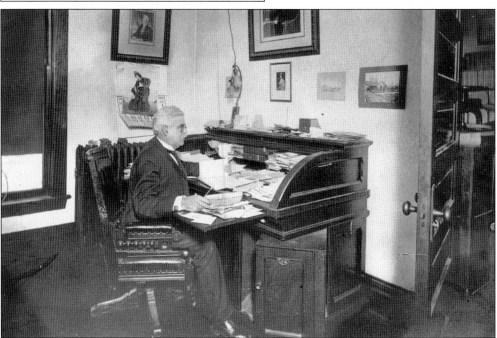

Walter Cooper originally opened Walter Cooper's Armory and Gun Manufactory in 1872, one of the first brick buildings in Bozeman. Black's Mercantile, a drugstore, and a market were also located in the building. Bozeman's earliest library was on the second floor.

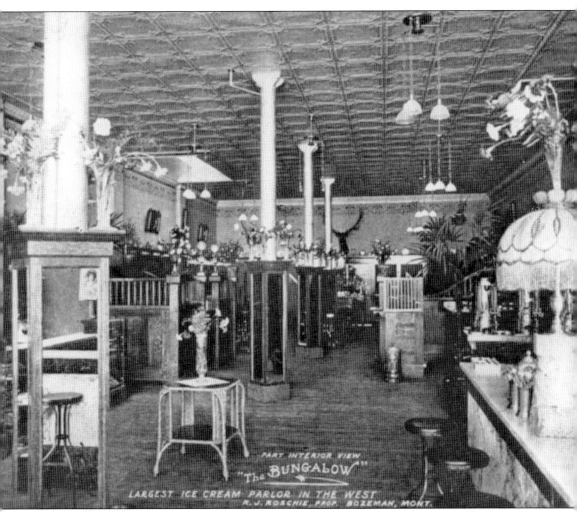

PART INTERIOR VIEW
"The BUNGALOW"
LARGEST ICE CREAM PARLOR IN THE WEST
R. J. ROSCHIE, PROP. BOZEMAN, MONT.

The Bungalow sold candy, chocolates, and ice cream in the early 1900s. Located next to the Rialto Theatre, it was a popular downtown gathering spot until it closed in 1994.

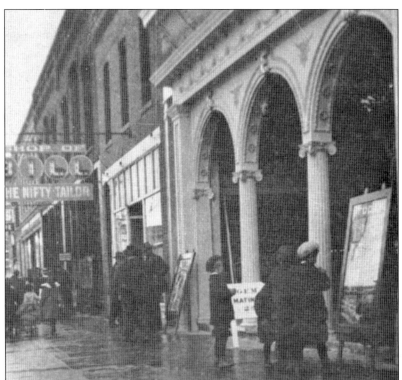

The Gem Theatre, pictured in 1914, was one of the many electric theaters in downtown Bozeman. As the market grew more competitive, theater owners added other incentives to attract patrons, such as a bowling alley and a pool hall.

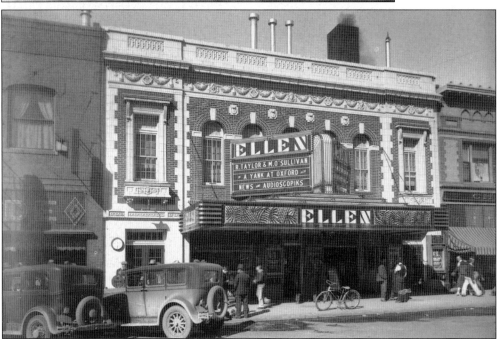

The more ornate Ellen Theatre was built in 1919 by Nelson and T. Byron Story to honor their mother. The theater, designed by architect Fred Willson, had a stage for live theater as well as a screen for movies. It had a banquet hall and a dance floor on the second floor. The Ellen featured musicals and the Bozeman Symphony Orchestra and had daily showings of movies until 2006.

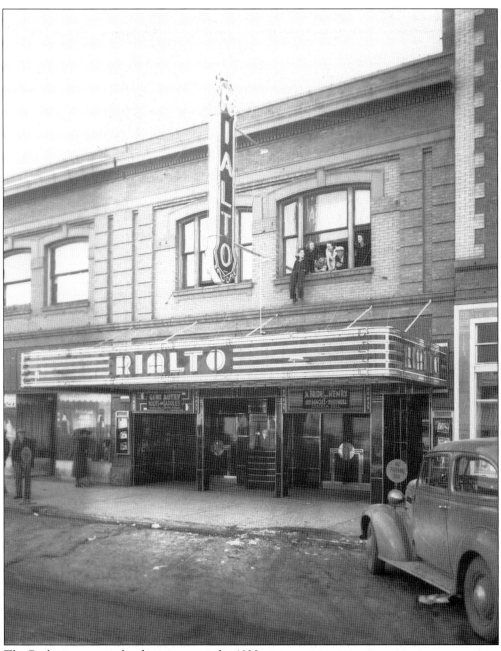

The Rialto was a popular downtown in the 1930s.

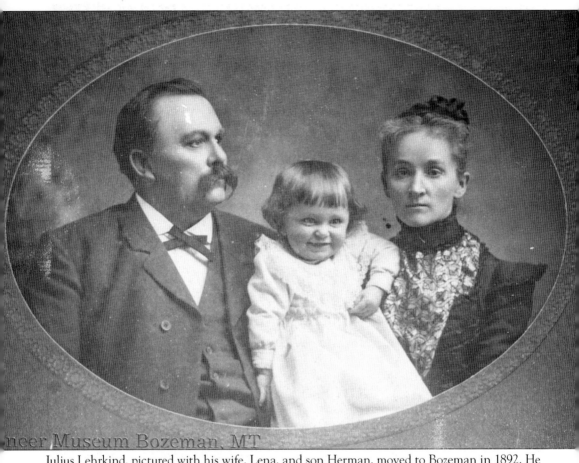

Julius Lehrkind, pictured with his wife, Lena, and son Herman, moved to Bozeman in 1892. He bought the Bozeman Brewing Company and built a new brewery near the railroad line.

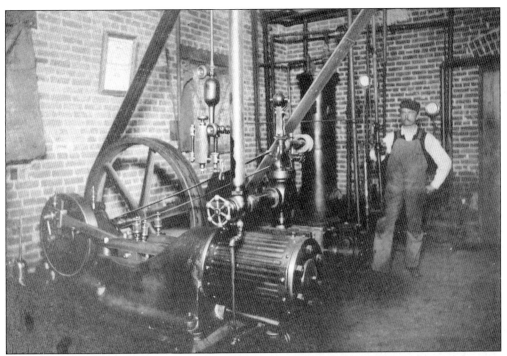

A workman stands watch over the Lehrkind Brewery engine room in 1898.

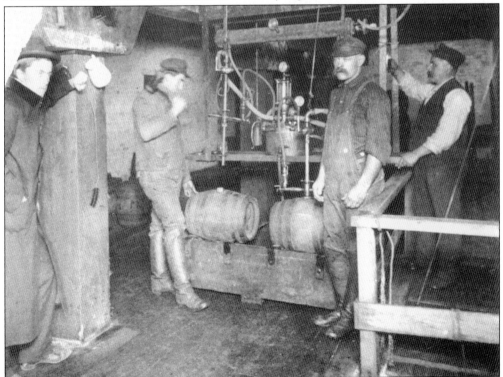

Lehrkind Brewery was a thriving business until Prohibition. The business managed to survive and today is a wholesale distributor of soft drinks, beer, and wine.

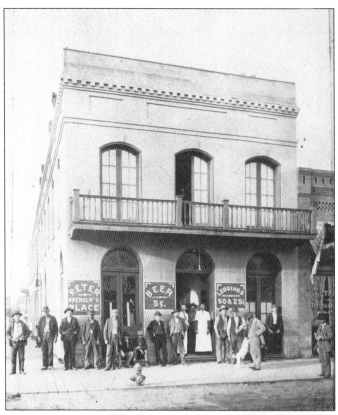

Once the Metropolitan Hotel, Peter Brenden's Place at the corner of Main Street and Bozeman Avenue served 5¢ beer and had accommodations available for 25¢ to 50¢ in 1907. Brenden is pictured at center in a black homburg.

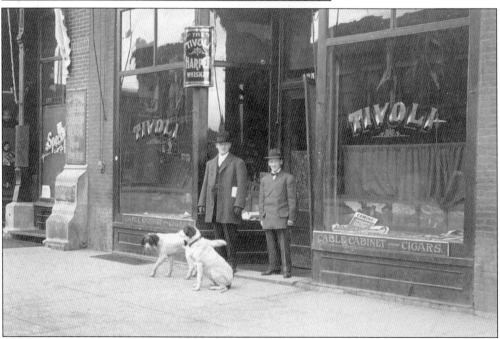

The Tivoli Saloon was a popular watering hole downtown. John Fechter (at left), his brother Heinie, and two of their canine friends are pictured c. 1910.

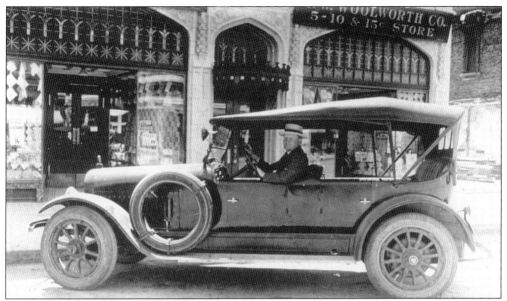

Businessman and entrepreneur John Fechter poses in his Super Six Hudson in front of the Fetcher Building on Main Street *c.* 1920. Architect Fred Willson designed the distinctive building in 1918. The building originally served as a hotel. Later F. W. Woolworth was a tenant, followed by J. C. Penney.

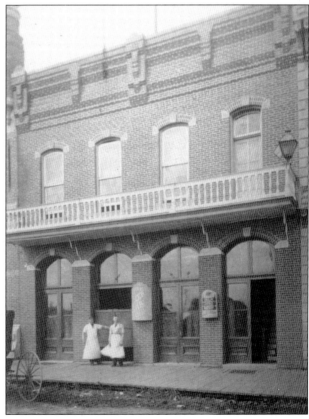

The building at 125 West Main Street once housed the Tivoli Beer Hall.

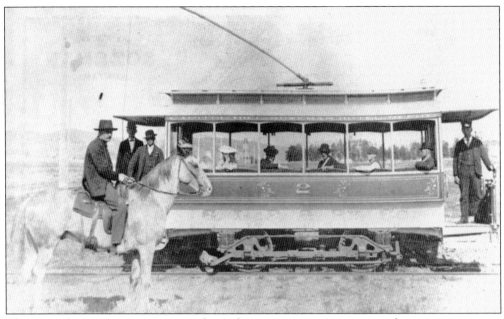

The interurban streetcars were a popular and convenient way to get around town.

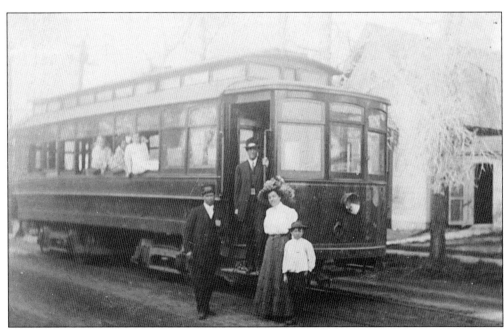

The streetcars had regular routes around Bozeman and also traveled all the way to Salesville (now Gallatin Gateway).

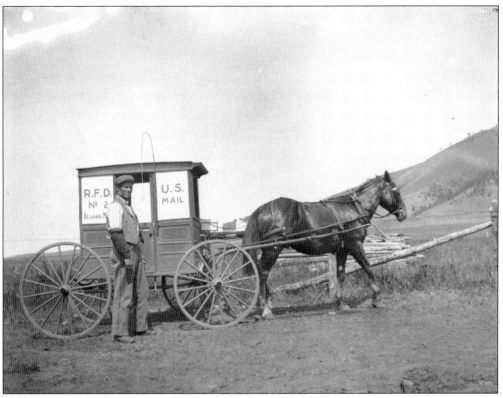

Mailman Henry Scheytt delivers the U.S. Mail in Belgrade.

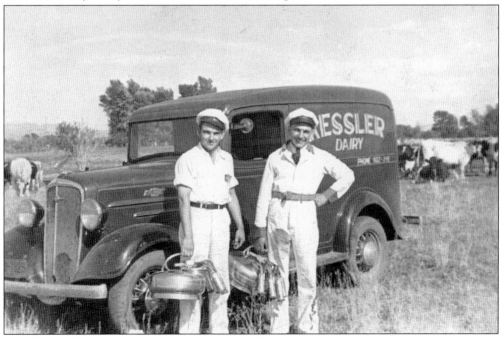

Arnold (at left) and Fred Kessler proudly pose in front of the first new delivery truck for Kessler Dairy in 1934.

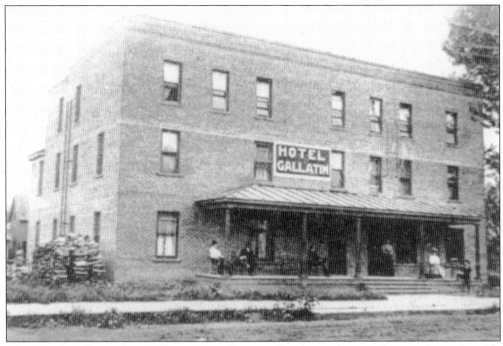

The Hotel Gallatin (c. 1905) on Main Street offered travelers modern and comfortable accommodations in Bozeman.

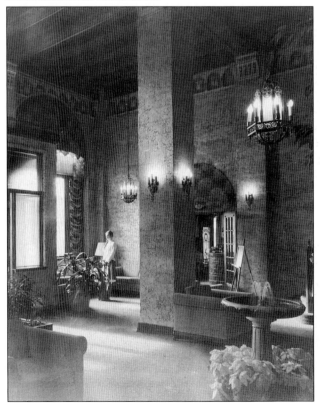

Designed by Fred Willson, the Baxter Hotel was an important addition to Bozeman's Main Street in 1929. The hotel's elegant lobby is pictured. Built to attract the growing number of tourists to the area, the Baxter Hotel is still a familiar landmark in 2008. One significant addition is a blue light on top of the building. The blue light flashes in winter to alert ski enthusiasts that snow is falling at nearby Bridger Bowl Ski Area.

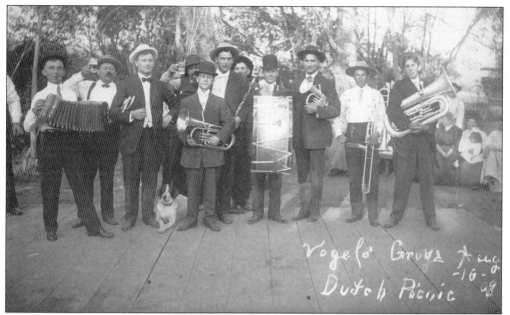

Bozeman residents were civic-minded individuals. Here the Bozeman Band is pictured on August 10, 1908. (Photograph by Schlechten Studio.)

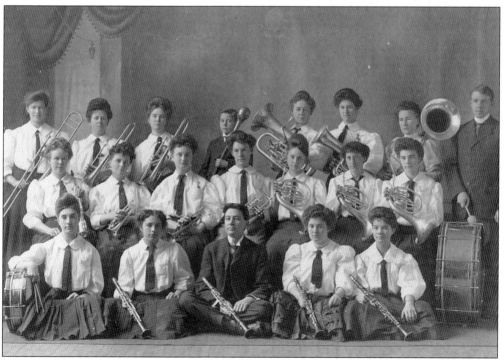

The Ladies Imperial Band, pictured in 1906, was particularly popular during the Sweet Pea Carnival Parade.

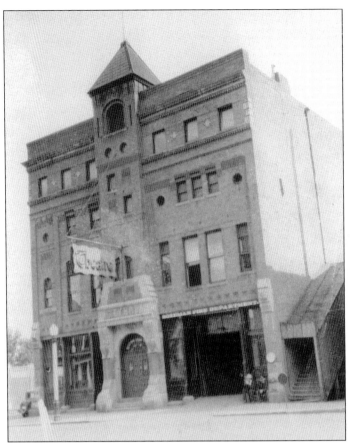

The Bozeman Opera House, located at the southwest corner of Rouse Avenue and Main Street, was a major project for downtown Bozeman. The ambitious project was planned to hold not only an elegant opera house but also the city necessities of fire and police departments, jail, and the library. After several years of planning, the building was completed in 1890. The opera house is pictured on June 26, 1929. It remained a prominent Bozeman landmark until it was demolished in 1965. A park is now located on the downtown corner where the opera house once stood.

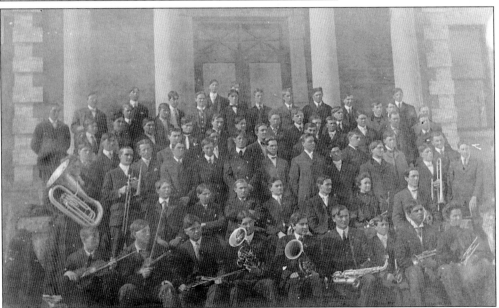

A band poses after a concert on the steps of the Carnegie Library, which was located at the corner or North Bozeman Avenue and Mendenhall Street.

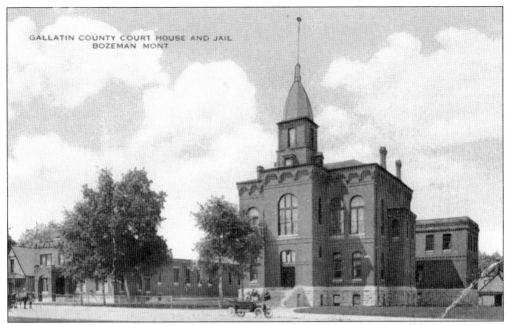

The Gallatin County Courthouse was built in 1880. The nearby jail was designed by Fred Willson and built in 1911 to meet the needs of the growing town. In 1979, the Gallatin Historical Society was given two rooms in the jail building. After the last prisoners were moved to the new jail facility in 1982, the county commissioners gave the Pioneer Museum the use of the entire building.

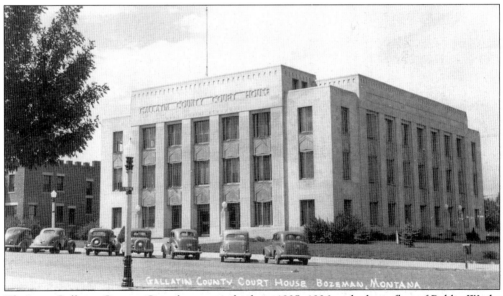

The new Gallatin County Courthouse was built in 1935–1936 with the influx of Public Works Administration money. Designed by Fred Willson, the new courthouse featured a less ornate design with clean, contemporary lines.

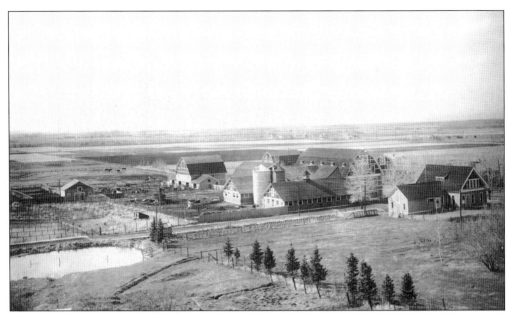

The farm for Agricultural College was located at Third Avenue and Lincoln Street on a 160-acre site donated by the county. The adjoining 40 acres, which had originally been designated as the state capitol site, was slated for the campus buildings. In the 1920s, the institution became known as Montana State College. In 1965, the legislature changed the name to Montana State University.

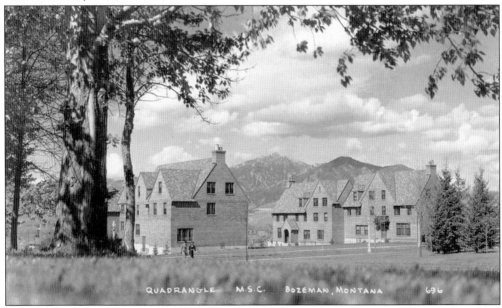

QUADRANGLE M.S.C. BOZEMAN, MONTANA 696

The Agricultural College of the State of Montana was founded on February 16, 1893, in Bozeman. The college was a consolation prize of sorts to the town, since it had been in the running with Helena, Anaconda, and Butte for the title of state capital. In anticipation, the capitol hill addition was planned, with Eighth Avenue slated as the main road leading to what they hoped would be the state capitol. Instead, the legislature apportioned the land grant college to Bozeman. Here the Quadrangle is pictured, which is near the intersection of Eighth Avenue and Cleveland Street.

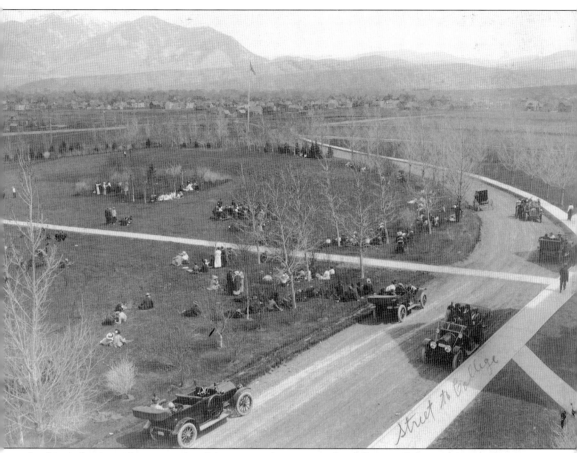

In this early view of campus, the elaborate road system to the college is shown.

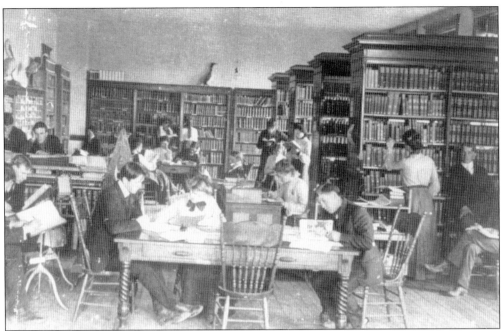

The first classes at the college were held in a roller skating rink located at Main Street and Third Avenue. The first-year class had 135 students. Later in 1898, Montana Hall, one of the main buildings on the new campus, was built. Students are pictured studying in the campus library in Montana Hall in 1904.

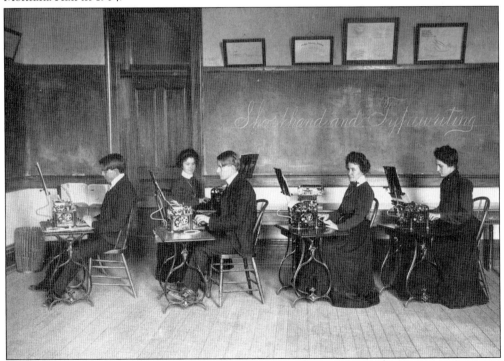

In this shorthand and typewriting class, *c.* 1900, students learn the fine art of dictation and transcription.

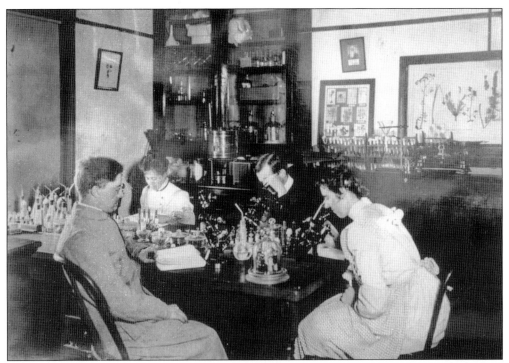

Freshman Beatrice Freeman Davis (at right) examines slides under a microscope in the biology lab in 1896.

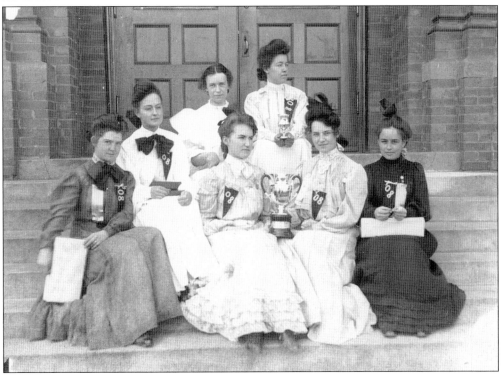

Women of the graduating class of 1908 pose on campus.

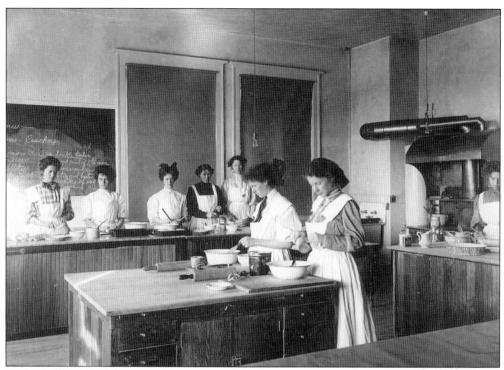

In the freshman home economics class, students hone their cooking skills around 1909.

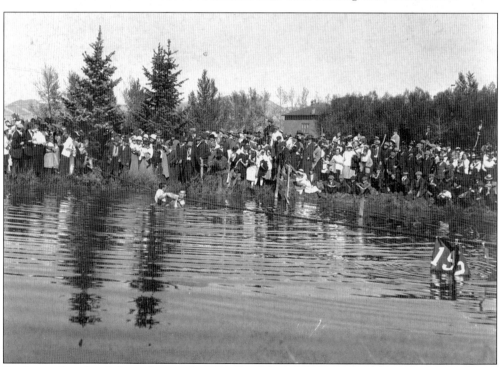

Students take a break from their studies for a bit of fun at the frog pond in 1916. The frog pond, located on Eleventh Avenue on today's campus, is now popularly known as the duck pond.

Seven

A LOVE OF FLOATS AND FLOWERS

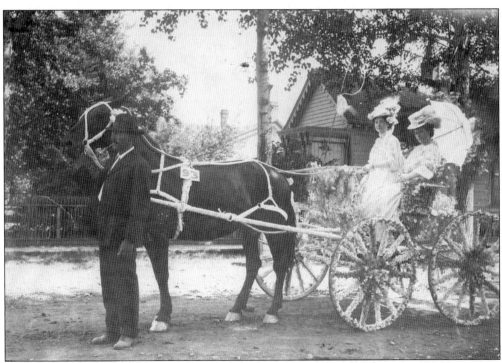

Astute Bozeman businessmen and merchants of the Commercial Club developed the idea of the Sweet Pea Carnival as a way to promote Bozeman and the Gallatin Valley. The first Sweet Pea Carnival was held on August 11, 1906, and lasted three days. A parade down Main Street kicked off the event. Here Anna Walsh (at left) and Helen Walsh Lutz prepare to ride in the parade.

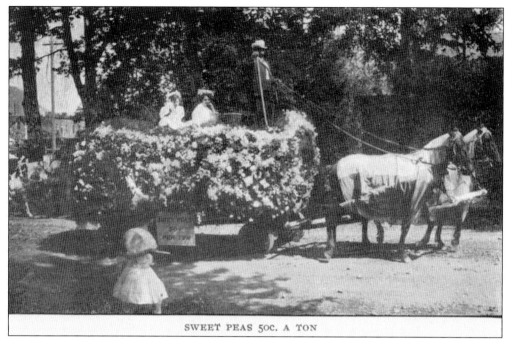

SWEET PEAS 50C. A TON

The sweet pea was chosen for the carnival symbol since it were readily available and bloomed fragrantly in August. A sign that aptly read "Sweet Peas 50 cents per ton" on this float summed up the abundance of the blossom.

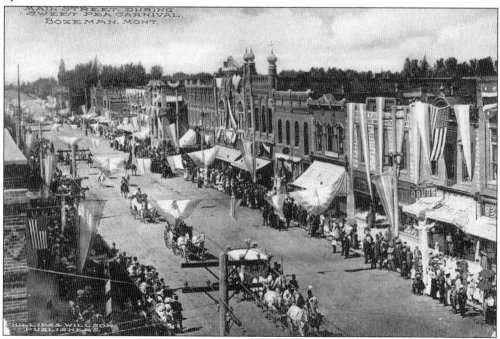

Carnival organizers modeled the festival on Mardi Gras in New Orleans and the Rose Festival in Portland, which they hoped would draw visitors to the area. R. D. Steele, who was in charge of the business end of the event, concluded that it would provide the "most free advertising imagined."

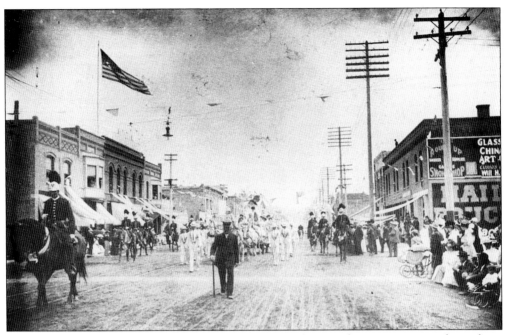

The first Sweet Pea Carnival included over 200 floats decorated in sweet peas and marching bands. Every business and home promised to participate in decorating the carriages and floats in a show of Bozeman's civic pride. The newspaper called on citizens to contribute sweet pea blossoms to decorate the floats.

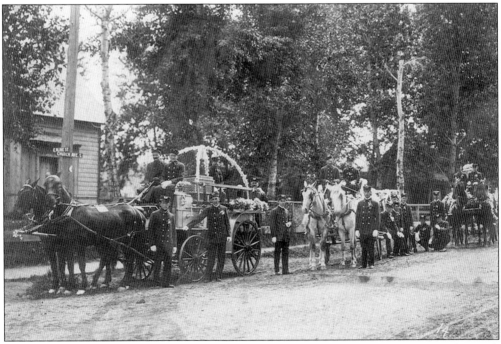

The Bozeman Fire Department stood ready for the parade at the corner of Olive Street and Church Avenue. Fire chief Alexander is seated on the right in the first wagon, while Harry Ferguson prepares to guide the float through the parade route.

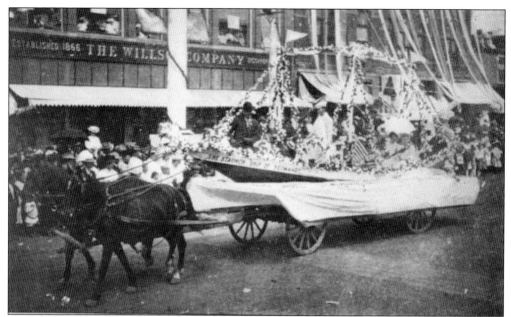

Newspaper accounts of the Sweet Pea Carnival deemed it a rousing success because of the united efforts of the citizens of Bozeman. The town was heartily congratulated on its patriotism. In the August 14, 1906, edition of the *Republican Courier*, R. D. Steele credited the women with decorating the private carriages and floats because "men do not know how."

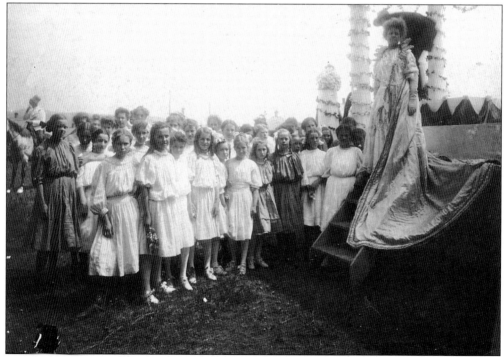

Kathryn Hanley was crowned the first queen of the Sweet Pea Carnival in a ceremony on the evening of August 10, 1906. Here Hanley poses in her queenly attire surrounded by a group of young girls who most likely hope to one day wear the royal regalia.

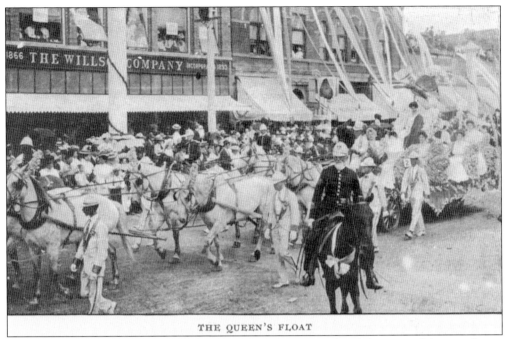

THE QUEEN'S FLOAT

The queen's float led the parade down Main Street. Her arrival and the start of the parade was heralded by a chorus of trumpets. Following the queen was a float carrying her court. Main Street businesses got into the spirit of the carnival by decorating with pink, white, and green bunting and festive pennants.

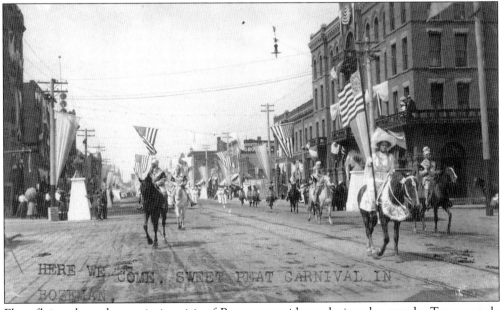

Flags flying show the patriotic spirit of Bozeman residents during the parade. Townspeople acknowledged after the first parade that dry and dusty Main Street needed to be paved. By 1909, the paved parade route made for much cleaner festivities.

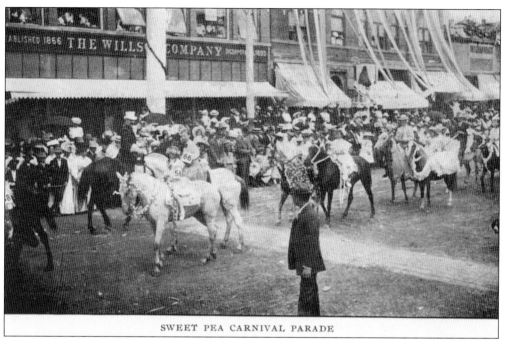

SWEET PEA CARNIVAL PARADE

The first parade was a rousing success but was not without incident. One man attempted to get his parade entry into the line-up at Main Street and Rouse Avenue even though law enforcement tried to prevent him from doing so. When he backed up, he set off a chain of unfortunate events, including bolting horses and parade participants being thrown to the ground. Amazingly, no one was seriously injured, and the parade continued without incident.

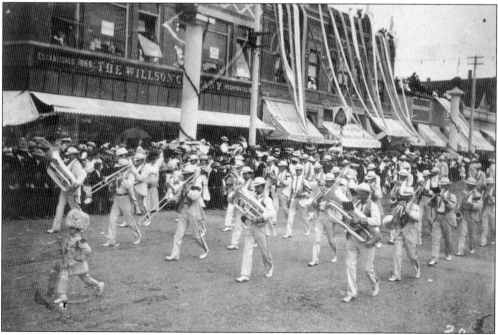

Every parade needs at least one marching band, and the Sweet Pea Carnival was no exception. Here the Bozeman Men's Band marches and plays lively tunes along the parade route.

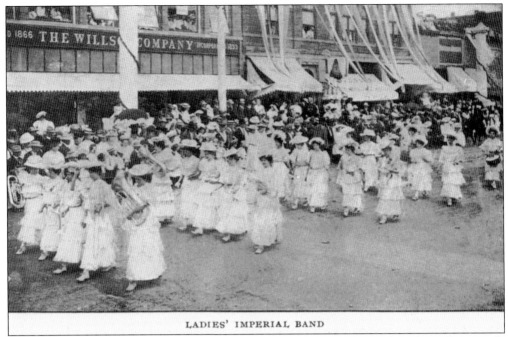

LADIES' IMPERIAL BAND

The popular Ladies Imperial Band was formed in late August 1906 and made its first parade appearance in 1907. The band marched the 24-block, unpaved parade route in their lovely white gowns while playing crowd-pleasing favorites.

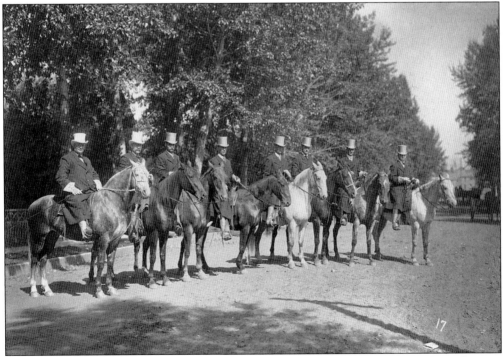

A group of men on horseback waiting for the start of the 1907 Sweet Pea Carnival parade poses wearing fancy top hats.

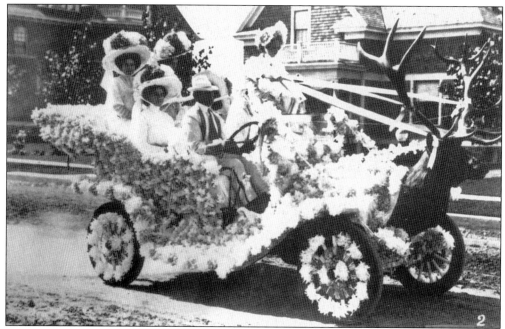

This 1907 parade entry added a unique western touch—elk horns. Nearly every inch of this car, including the tires, was elaborately festooned with thousands of delicate sweet pea blossoms. Driver Frank Esgar escorts the elegantly dressed women whose hats are decorated, of course, with fragrant flowers.

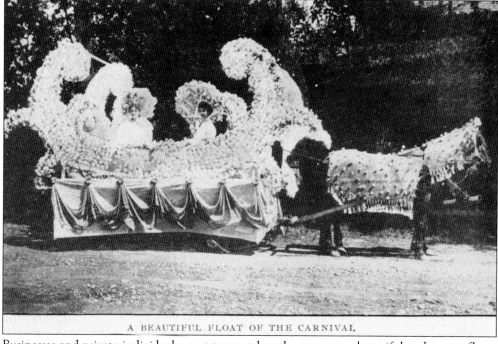

A BEAUTIFUL FLOAT OF THE CARNIVAL

Businesses and private individuals went to great lengths to prepare beautiful and ornate floats each year. Riders in the floats were bedecked in an equally stunning display of floral artistry. Even the horse pulling this stunning float was adorned in a decorative blanket.

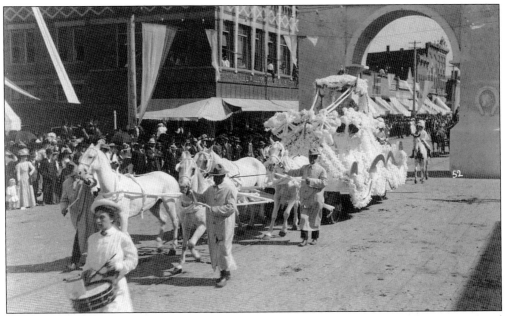

In 1909, the Sweet Pea Parade passed through a large archway at Main Street and Black Avenue.

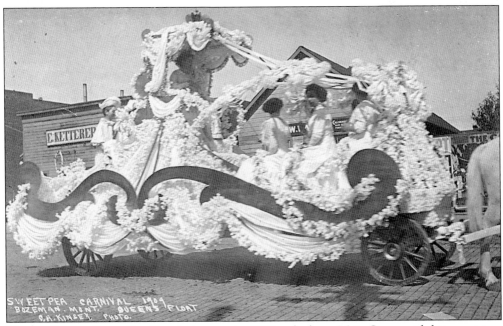

Miriam Cooper, Sweet Pea Carnival queen in 1909, rode down Main Street with her court in a display of pageantry befitting royalty.

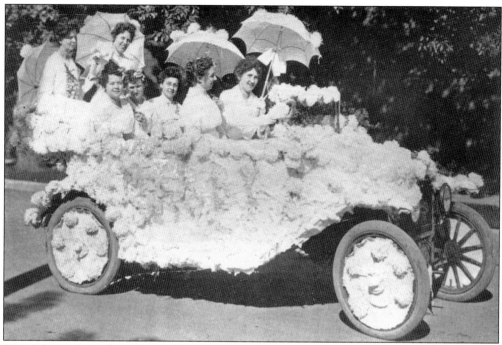

From left to right in the 1909 parade, Fanny Jacobs Cowan, Ruth Dagget Bartholomew, Pearl Haley Bell, Cora Jarvis, Gertie Hays, Hattie Taber Letts, and Grace Marios kept with the floral theme but broke tradition by decorating their vehicle with chrysanthemums instead of sweet peas.

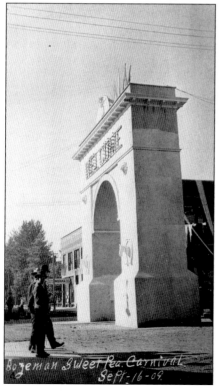

A large "Welcome" arch was constructed on Main Street for the parade route in 1909.

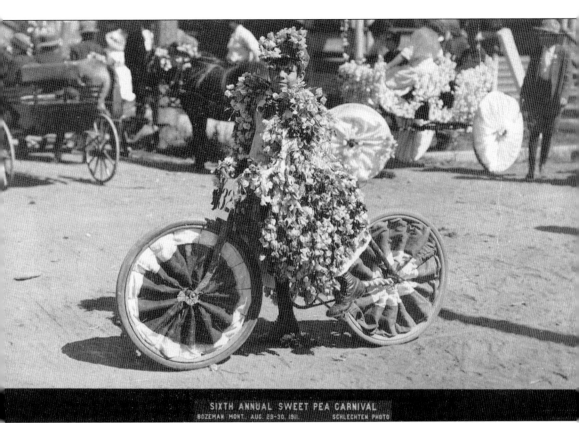

SIXTH ANNUAL SWEET PEA CARNIVAL
BOZEMAN MONT. AUG. 29-30, 1911.   SCHLECHTEN PHOTO

Years after the first carnival, everyone was still smitten with the Sweet Pea Carnival and its festivities. Townspeople got into the spirit of the carnival by decorating everything from wagons to sheep with flowers and crepe paper. William "Willie" Watts dressed in an enormous cloak of sweet pea blossoms as he prepared to ride his bicycle in the sixth annual parade in 1911. (Photograph by Schlechten Studio.)

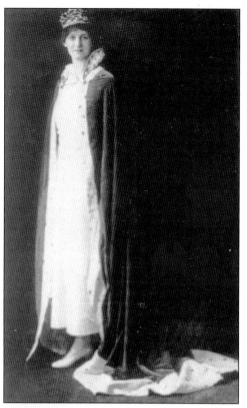

Despite eight years of unbridled enthusiasm for the Sweet Pea Carnival and its festivities, no carnival was held in 1914. Many were worried about the war in Europe, and a blight decimated the sweet pea crop that year. In 1916, townspeople attempted to revive the carnival, and Lela Maxwell was crowned queen. Sadly it was the last Sweet Pea Festival held. In 1978, the spirit of the original carnival was honored with the first Sweet Pea Festival of the Arts, held in Lindley Park, which showcased local artisans. Each August, the festival remains a popular event.

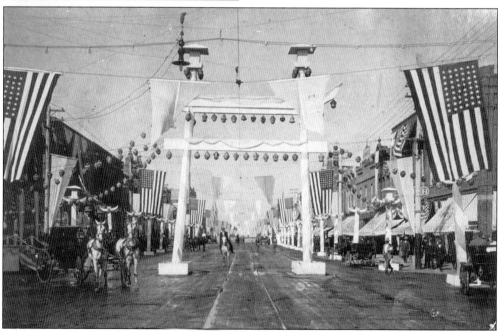

Bozemanites loved their parades, no matter the reason, and took pride in creating a festive and patriotic setting for events such as Montana Day, Pioneer Parade, Roundup, and the Fourth of July.

Eight

COWBOYS AND COWGIRLS

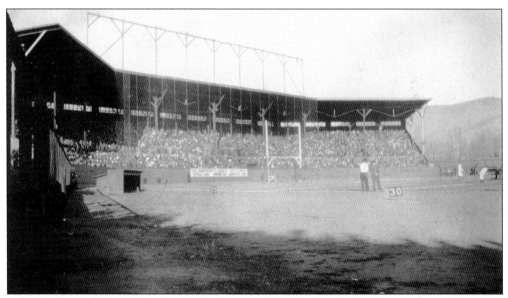

The first Bozeman Roundup was held August 12–14, 1919, in conjunction with the Montana Elks convention. T. B. Story, Nelson Story Jr., R. P McClelland, and Lester Work provided the financial backing for the venture. The group purchased a four-block tract of land between Tracy and Grand Avenues north of Main Street, where a grandstand, racetrack, and rodeo arena were built. Construction began on July 14, 1919, and was miraculously completed the night before the mid-August opening.

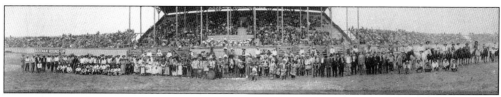

Bozeman Roundup participants (pictured in 1926) pose in front of the grandstands. The event drew performers from the national rodeo circuit to compete for cash prizes. With events ranging from bulldogging to trick riding to fancy roping, the Bozeman Roundup lived up to its concise slogan "She's Wild." (Photograph by R. R. Doubleday.)

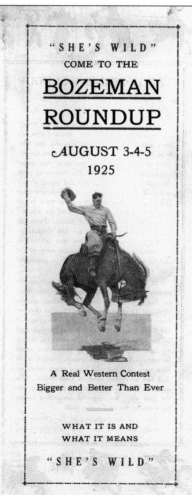

cattle was the establishment of the Brahma cattle of today, some of the best representatives of which you will see in their wild state in the Arena. They have an exceedingly tough hide and marvelous constitution and have developed into the most wonderful fighting steers in the world. Their main ambition in life seems to be to fight any man on foot and in order to protect the contestants from serious injury all of the Brahma steers used in the Bozeman Roundup have brass knobs placed on the ends of their horns.

Bozeman has the advantage of being located on the Yellowstone Trail near the Yellowstone Park, which fact is taken advantage of by thousands of visitors to the National Parks, who also arrange to visit the Roundup at this time. Bozeman is the entrance to the Yellowstone Park via the scenic Gallatin Way, and is but twenty-five miles from Livingston, the entrance to the Park via Gardiner. In addition, Bozeman is served by the Northern Pacific and the Chicago, Milwaukee and St. Paul Railroads.

THREE DAYS OF THRILLING WESTERN SPORTS

Vast Arena has Seating Capacity of 20,000

SEVENTH ANNUAL ROUNDUP BOZEMAN, MONTANA

August 3, 4, 5, 1925

Bozeman Chronicle Print

"SHE'S WILD"
COME TO THE

BOZEMAN
ROUNDUP

AUGUST 3-4-5
1925

A Real Western Contest
Bigger and Better Than Ever

WHAT IT IS AND
WHAT IT MEANS

"SHE'S WILD"

The Bozeman Roundup brought forth the spirit of the Old West. In the past, riders would gather for sport and fun to show their skills. The Roundup honored that essence of the true cowboys and cowgirls.

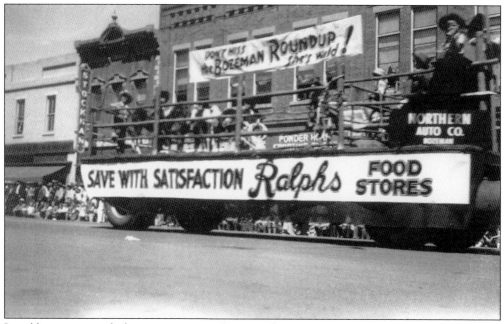

Local businesses took the opportunity to decorate floats as part of the Roundup Parade. Ralph's Food Store float points out its great savings for consumers during the parade.

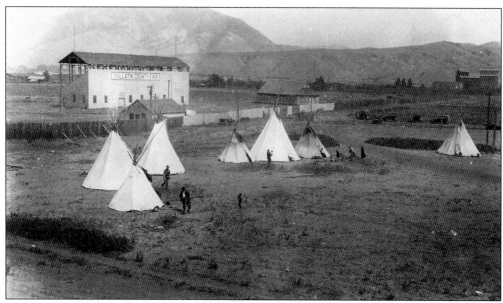

Native Americans from the Flathead reservation came to participate in the Bozeman Roundup. Native Americans camped in their traditional tepees just behind the grandstands, c. 1918–1923.

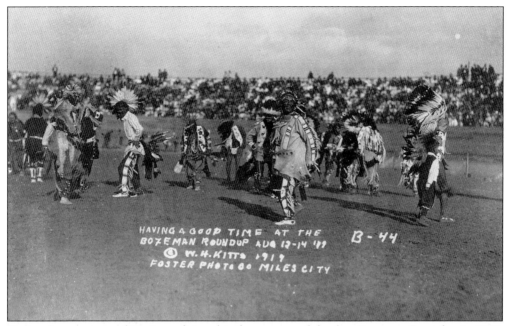

Native Americans perform in traditional garb as a part of the first Bozeman Roundup in 1919. (Photograph by W. H. Kitts, Foster Photo, Miles City, Montana.)

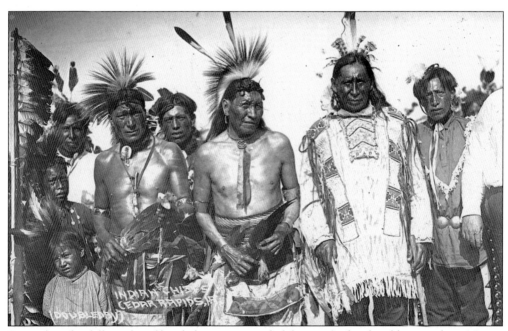

Dressed in the full regalia of beaded garments and elaborate feather headdresses, these Native Americans are from Cedar Rapids. (Photograph by R. R. Doubleday.)

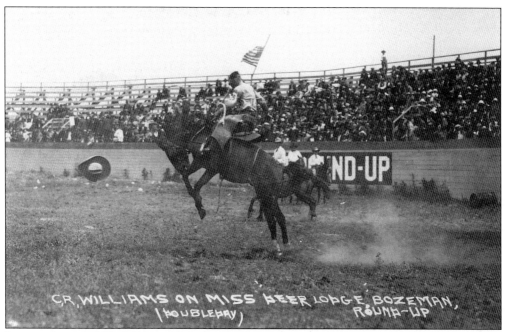

In its early years, the Bozeman Roundup displayed the talents of cowboys and cowgirls on the national rodeo circuit. They competed for part of the $6,000 purse. Trick and fancy roping, bareback riding, and bulldogging were just a few of the events that dazzled spectators during the festivities. Pictured is C. R. Williams riding Miss Deer Lodge. (Photograph by R. R. Doubleday.)

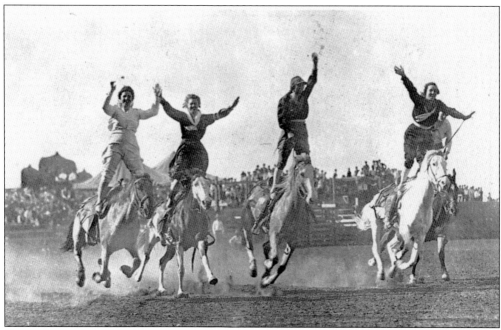

Cowgirls in the Hippodrome pose ride toward the Roundup c. 1921. (Photograph by R. R. Doubleday.)

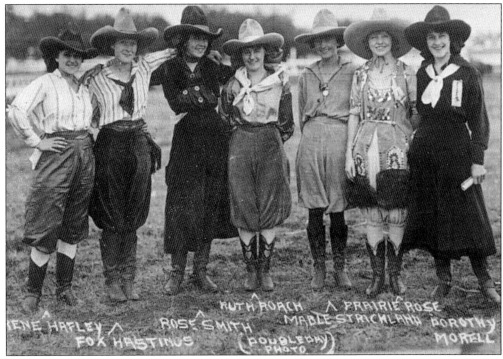

These cowgirls strike a proud pose during the 1920 Roundup. From left to right are Rene Hafley, Fox Hastings, Rose Smith, Ruth Roach, Mabel Strickland, Prairie Rose Henderson, and Dorothy Morrell. (Photograph by R. R. Doubleday.)

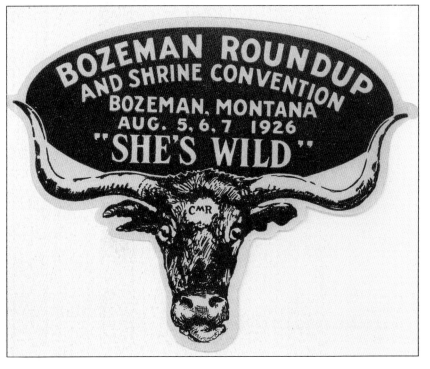

A sticker from the last Bozeman Roundup and Shrine Convention in 1926 was a small memento of the event.

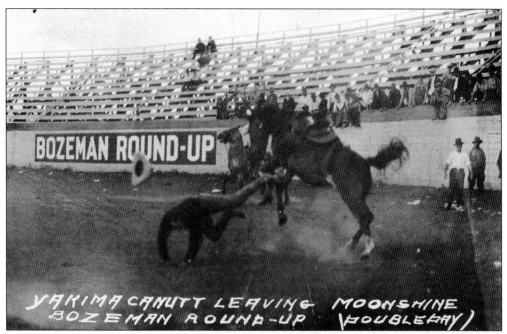

Riders faced the perils and dangers inherent in such activities. Here Yakima Canutt is pictured leaving Moonshine at the 1919 Roundup. (Photograph by R. R. Doubleday.)

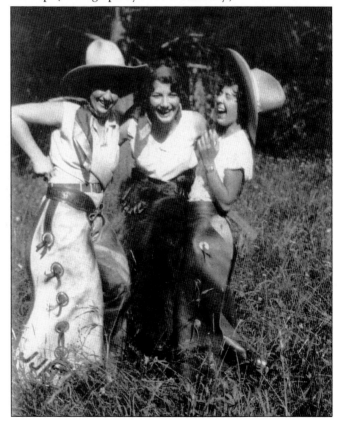

Although the names of these happy cowgirls are unknown, it is certain that they embody the spirit and independence of Montana women.

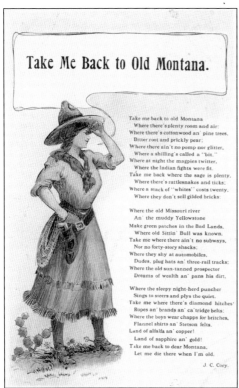

Take Me Back to Old Montana.

Take me back to old Montana
  Where there's plenty room and air:
Where there's cottonwood an' pine trees,
  Bitter root and prickly pear;
Where there ain't no pomp nor glitter,
  Where a shilling's called a "bit,"
Where at night the magpies twitter,
  Where the Indian fights were fit.
Take me back where the sage is plenty,
  Where there's rattlesnakes and ticks;
Where a stack of "whites" costs twenty,
  Where they don't sell gilded bricks;

Where the old Missouri river
  An' the muddy Yellowstone
Make green patches in the Bad Lands,
  Where old Sittin' Bull was known.
Take me where there ain't no subways,
  Nor no forty-story shacks;
Where they shy at automobiles,
  Dudes, plug hats an' three-rail tracks;
Where the old sun-tanned prospector
  Dreams of wealth an' pans his dirt.

Where the sleepy night-herd puncher
  Sings to steers and plys the quirt.
Take me where there's diamond hitches'
  Ropes an' brands an' ca'tridge belts;
Where the boys wear chapps for britches,
  Flannel shirts an' Stetson felts.
Land of alfalfa an' copper!
  Land of sapphire an' gold!
Take me back to dear Montana,
  Let me die there when I'm old.

                              J. C. Cory.

A postcard with the poem "Take Me Back to Old Montana" by J. C. Cory chronicles a love of life in the Old West.

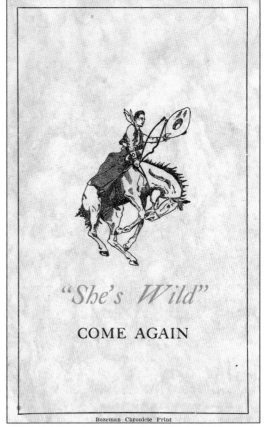

"She's Wild"

COME AGAIN

Bozeman Chronicle Print

The back page from a Roundup program sums it up well.

Nine

THE CALL OF THE WILD

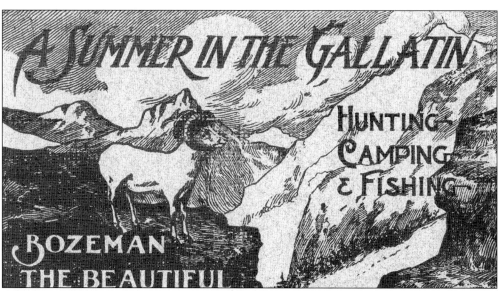

A brochure dubbed it "Bozeman the Beautiful" and invited visitors to enjoy hunting, camping, and fishing during a summer in the Gallatin Valley.

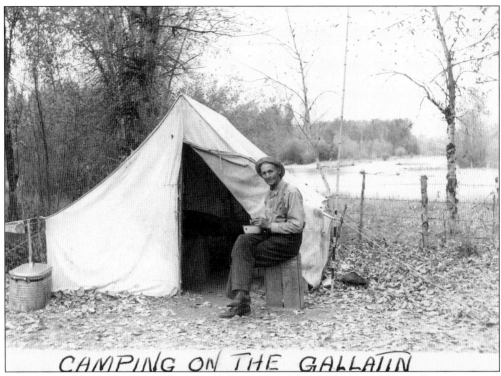

CAMPING ON THE GALLATIN

This unnamed gentleman enjoys a peaceful campsite along the banks of the Gallatin River.

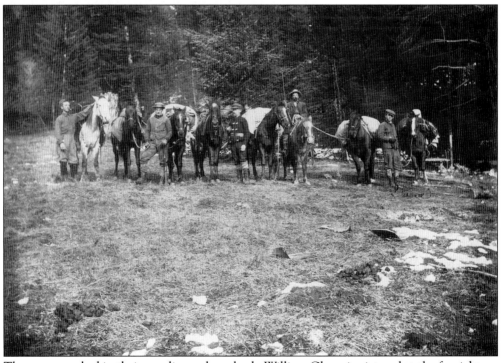

These men packed in their supplies on horseback. William Glawe is pictured at the far right.

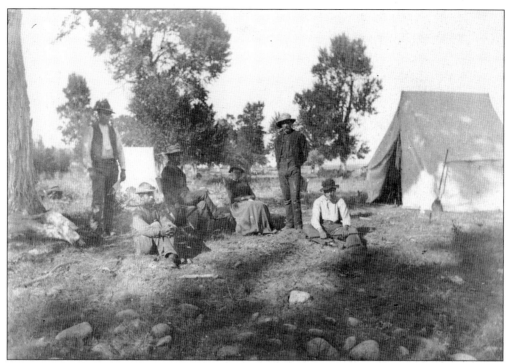

Camping has long been popular in the Gallatin Valley, with the beautiful mountains, clear streams, and clean air.

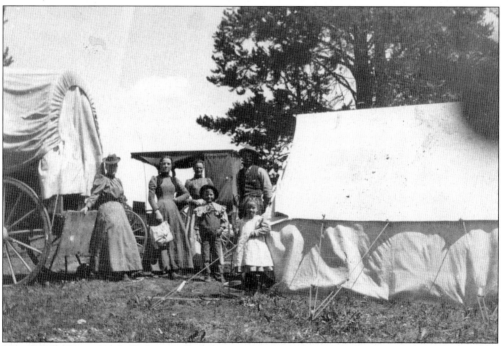

Mary Wells Yates (far left), later called Granny Yates, and company are on a camping trip. The widow Yates moved to the Dry Creek area, just north of Bozeman, in 1875. Many descendants of Yates still live in the area.

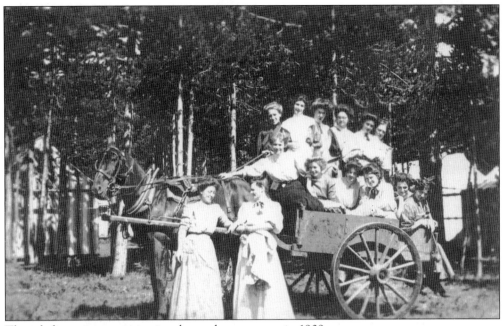

These ladies enjoy an outing in a horse-drawn wagon in 1909.

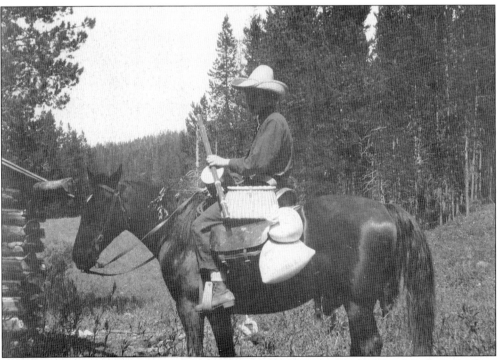

A fisherman in Hyalite Canyon reached the ranger station near Hyalite Creek on horseback, *c.* 1915. The rivers and streams of the Gallatin Valley have long provided residents with opportunities for outdoor recreation, including outstanding trout fishing.

The bicycle was popular in Bozeman. Here William Ginn is pictured training for a bicycle race.

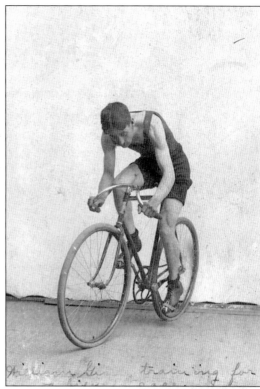

Montana women were uniquely independent and not restrained by conventional thinking. These two unnamed women enjoy a bicycle ride in 1906.

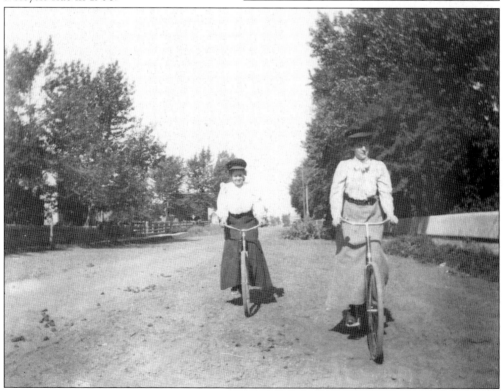

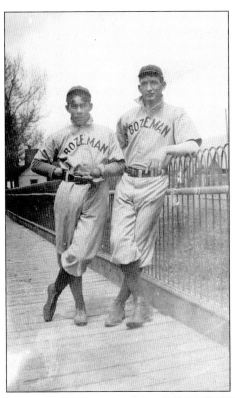

Baseball was a popular pastime in Bozeman. In conjunction with the first Sweet Pea Carnival festivities, a baseball game was scheduled between the Bozeman and Livingston teams competing for a $100 prize. The Bozeman team was victorious in 1906.

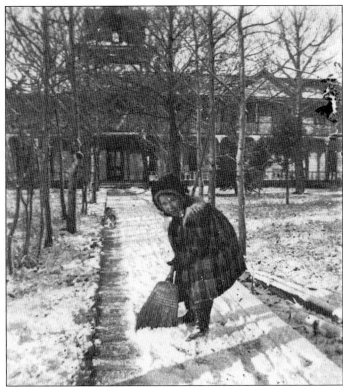

A child sweeps the snowy walk in front of Ferris Hot Springs. Today it operates as Bozeman Hot Springs, just west of town.

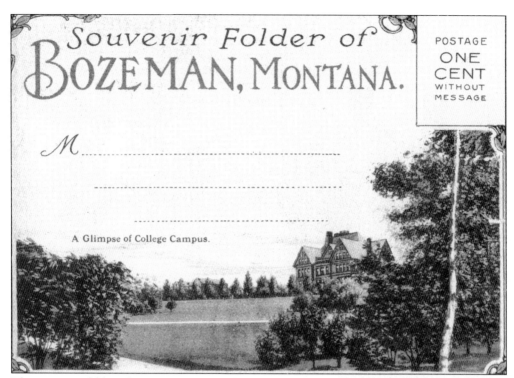

Souvenir Folder of

BOZEMAN, MONTANA.

M _____

_____

_____

A Glimpse of College Campus.

This souvenir folder of Bozeman contained scenic images, presumably to entice visitors.

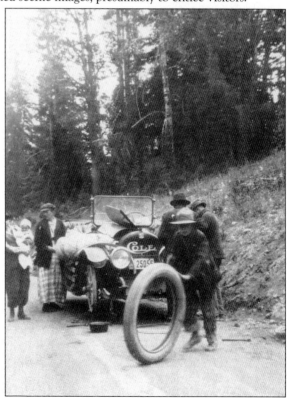

Even the hardship of having to stop to change a tire on their Cole Touring Car in 1914 does not detract from the enjoyment of the Benolken family on a trip to Yellowstone National Park.

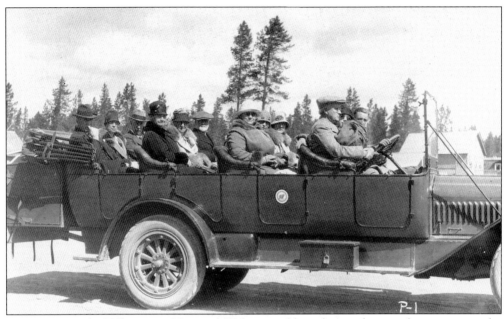

Visitors to nearby Yellowstone National Park were able to be up close to the scenery in the open car.

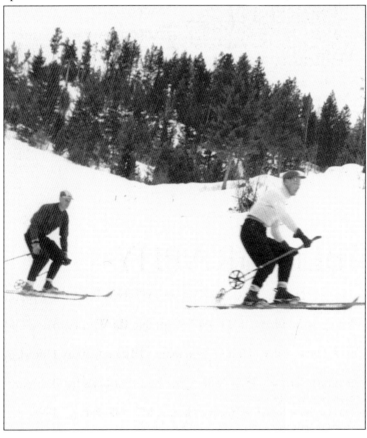

Dave Kundert, at right, skis popular Bear Canyon. Long winters and ample snows in the mountains surrounding Bozeman provided the opportunity for downhill skiing. Comfortable temperatures, sunny days, and deep snowpack created excellent skiing conditions long into spring months. Night skiing also became popular in the Bear Canyon ski area, where skiers placed railroad flares to light the part of the ski run.

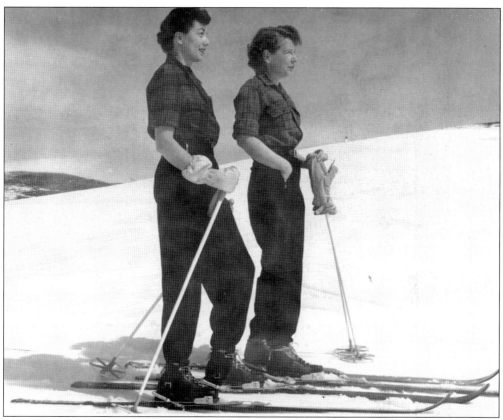

Marga Hosaeus and Gertrude Roskie enjoy a spring day on the slopes. Residents with pine skis and bamboo poles had to herringbone climb up the hill for the ride down. To eliminate the difficult climb, ski enthusiasts later used an old car motor to create a ski rope tow.

BIBLIOGRAPHY

Burlingame, M. G. *Gallatin County's Heritage: A Report of Progress 1805–1976*. Bozeman: Gallatin County Bicentennial Publication, 1976.

Leeson, Michael. A., ed. *History of Montana, 1739–1885*. Chicago, IL: Warner, Beers, and Company, 1885.

Rust, Thomas, ed. *Fort Ellis: A Documentary History*. Bozeman: Gallatin County Historical Society, 2004.

Seibel, Dennis. *Fort Ellis, Montana Territory 1867–1886*. "The Fort that Guarded Bozeman." Bozeman: Gallatin Historical Society, 1996.

Smith, Phyllis. *Bozeman and the Gallatin Valley, a History*. Helena, MT: Falcon Press, 1996.

———. *Sweet Pea Days, a History*. Bozeman: Artcraft Printing, 1997.

ACROSS AMERICA, PEOPLE ARE DISCOVERING
SOMETHING WONDERFUL. *THEIR HERITAGE.*

Arcadia Publishing is the leading local history publisher in the United States.
With more than 4,000 titles in print and hundreds of new titles released every
year, Arcadia has extensive specialized experience chronicling the history of
communities and celebrating America's hidden stories, bringing to life the people,
places, and events from the past. To discover the history of other communities
across the nation, please visit:

www.arcadiapublishing.com

Customized search tools allow you to find regional history books about the town
where you grew up, the cities where your friends and family live, the town where
your parents met, or even that retirement spot you've been dreaming about.

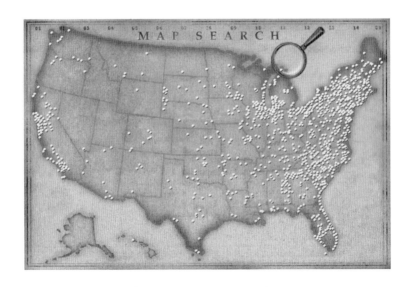